5: PERSPECTIVES IN CRITICISM

PERSPECTIVES IN CRITICISM

CHARLES MOORMAN

Arthurian Triptych

MYTHIC MATERIALS IN CHARLES WILLIAMS,
C. S. LEWIS, AND T. S. ELIOT

UNIVERSITY OF CALIFORNIA PRESS
Berkeley and Los Angeles
1960

University of California Press
Berkeley and Los Angeles, California
Cambridge University Press
London, England

LIBRARY OF CONGRESS CATALOG CARD NUMBER: 59-14476
Printed in the United States of America
Designed by Ward Ritchie

For Ruth

Acknowledgments

I AM HAPPY for the privilege of acknowledging in print a few of the many debts and obligations I have incurred in the writing of this study.

My friends at Tulane—Richard H. Fogle, R. M. Lumiansky, Aline Mackenzie Taylor, Dick Taylor, Jr., and William S. Woods—have for years listened patiently to all my problems and have given generously of their wisdom and experience. They may well claim credit for the best of what is said here, and I hope that my own shortcomings will not embarrass them.

To Roger P. McCutcheon, Dean Emeritus of the Tulane Graduate School, I owe a special debt for his unfailing encouragement of my work and for his kindly concern for me and my family. I regret that this book can be only in "partial fulfillment" of my many obligations to him.

Professor Malcolm F. McGregor of the University of British Columbia has been a continuing source of inspiration and advice, and whatever I do owes much to him.

I should like to thank also Professor C. S. Lewis for his generous replies to my queries. The editors and staff of the University of California Press have guided me with courtesy through the process of publication. Miss Maudell Fairchild, Miss Marilyn Lane, and Mrs. Carolyn Yates have assisted cheerfully with typing and editorial problems.

For permission to quote copyrighted material, I wish to express my thanks to:

G. Bell and Sons, Ltd. for the quotation from *The Quest of the Holy Grail* by Jessie L. Weston.

Geoffrey Bles, Ltd. for quotations from *Till We Have Faces, Mere Christianity,* and *Miracles* by C. S. Lewis.

Cambridge University Press for the quotation from *From Ritual to Romance* by Jessie L. Weston.

Faber and Faber, Ltd. for quotations from *Descent into Hell, The Descent of the Dove, The Figure of Beatrice, He Came Down From Heaven,* and *The Forgiveness of Sins* by Charles Williams; and from " 'Ulysses,' Order, and Myth" by T. S. Eliot.

Harcourt, Brace and Company, Inc. for quotations from *After Strange Gods* by T. S. Eliot, copyright, 1934, by Harcourt, Brace and Company, Inc.; from *Four Quartets* by T. S. Eliot, copyright, 1943, by T. S. Eliot, reprinted by permission of Harcourt, Brace and Company, Inc.—for "The Dry Salvages" extract; from *Collected Poems 1909–1935* by T. S. Eliot, copyright, 1936, by Harcourt, Brace and Company, Inc. and reprinted with their permission—for "The Waste Land," "Sweeney" and "Prufrock" quotes; and from *Selected Essays of T. S. Eliot,* copyright 1932, 1936, 1950 by Harcourt, Brace and Company, Inc. and reprinted with their permission.

Harper and Brothers for quotations from *Language and Myth* by Ernst Cassirer.

The editors of *The Kenyon Review* for the quotation from Stanley Edgar Hyman's "Myth, Ritual, and Nonsense."

The Macmillan Company for quotations from *Collected Poems* by W. B. Yeats (copyright, 1954); and from *Out of the Silent Planet, Perelandra,* and *That Hideous Strength* by C. S. Lewis.

The Executive Secretary of The Modern Language Association of America for the quotation from William A. Nitze's "The Fisher King in the Grail Romances."

Oxford University Press for quotations from *Arthurian Torso* by Charles Williams and C. S. Lewis; from "The World's Classics" edition of *The English Poems of John Milton;* from *Taliessin Through Logres* and *The Region of the Summer Stars* by Charles Williams; and from *The Allegory of Love* by C. S. Lewis.

Prentice-Hall, Inc. for the quotation from *Modern Poetry,* edited by Maynard Mack, Leonard Dean, and William Frost.

Portions of chapters 3, 4, and 5 have appeared as articles in *Modern Fiction Studies, College English,* and *The South Atlantic Quarterly* and are reprinted here with the permission of the editors of those journals.

The letter from C. S. Lewis is quoted with his permission.

The dedication page, however, records the greatest and happiest debt that I have.

C. M.

Contents

Titles of Abbreviated Sources

Lewis

AT   *Arthurian Torso*. London: Oxford University Press, 1948.

HS   *That Hideous Strength*. New York: Macmillan, 1946.

PE   *Perelandra*. New York: Macmillan, 1944.

SP   *Out of the Silent Planet*. New York: Macmillan, 1943.

Williams

AT   *Arthurian Torso* [*The Figure of Arthur*]. London: Oxford University Press, 1948.

DIH   *Descent into Hell*. London: Faber, 1937.

SS   *The Region of the Summer Stars*. London: Oxford University Press, 1955.

TTL   *Taliessin Through Logres*. London: Oxford University Press, 1955.

1

Myth and Modern Literature

In a paper delivered at the 1956 meeting of the Modern Language Association, Philip Young named as a major trend in modern criticism the "rush to get on the Myth Bandwagon." And as long ago as 1949, Stanley Edgar Hyman began an article entitled "Myth, Ritual, and Nonsense" with the statement that "myth is the new intellectual fashion, apparently, and judging by the recent books on the subject, there is more than one way to skin a myth."[1] Quite obviously we are already in the midst of a new literary and critical movement, undefined as yet, but certainly perceptible in the new books and in the journals; the field of myth study has in recent years become as intense and as cluttered a battleground as was the New Criticism in the early days of *The Southern Review*. Moreover, the combatants are now more varied; anthropologists, folklorists, psychologists, sociologists, linguists, and historians, as well as literary scholars of every variety, have found bright new axes to grind in the open game of myth hunting.

Although there is as yet no real "mythological" school of criticism, there are certainly great numbers of individual mythological critics, exhibiting a considerable diversity in range and approach. One finds, for example, Richard Chase (an anthropologist) working on Melville,[2] Stith Thompson (a folklorist)[3] and R.

W. B. Lewis (a ritualist)[4] interpreting American literature, Maud Bodkin (a Jungian) explaining *Paradise Lost*,[5] Ernest Jones (a Freudian) investigating *Hamlet*,[6] Francis Fergusson (a ritualist) interpreting drama,[7] Philip Wheelwright (a semanticist) explaining the *Oresteia*,[8] and C. L. Barber (a ritualist) investigating Shakespeare[9]—all in terms of mythical situations and patterns. And this list could, without difficulty, be extended enormously.[10]

That there is a new and important myth consciousness manifesting itself in all fields of literary endeavor we can document quantitatively. An explanation of this phenomenon, however, demands another sort of evidence. This change in outlook toward myth can be explained in two sets of terms—psychological and historical. Psychologically, the present interest in myth reflects a need and a search for order and certainty in the midst of the apparent chaos and disorder of the twentieth century. It is no accident that the three writers with whom this study deals did most of their writing in the hectic years between two wars, in the years when the memory of the old war was too fresh to be forgotten and the possibility of a new war too immediate to be ignored. The literature of these interbellum years is filled with a yearning for order, for a way out of what Eliot called a waste land and Gertrude Stein a lost generation. Order was sought everywhere; Hemingway sought it in the strong man's allegiance to a tough code, Faulkner in a reassertion of the values, if not the system, of an aristocratic society, Eliot, Graham Greene, Auden, Evelyn Waugh, and Aldous Huxley in strongly conservative and patterned religious groups. Thus it is that poets have stepped outside the contemporary scene into a world of myth, a world that contains order and meaning within itself. Myth offers the poet a complete and ordered cosmos, an irreducible system of coherent belief upon which he can construct an ordered and meaningful poetry. Certainly the major

2

and universally accepted symbols of our daily life—
tired blood, the atom bomb, the supermarket—do not
have in them the makings of great poetry; the world of
myth, on the other hand, provides a meaningful and
coherent symbolism upon which the poet may draw.

That despair and frustration may at least partly account for the new interest in myth is necessarily difficult to demonstrate; the historical process that leads to
this myth consciousness in literature may be traced
with somewhat more precision. Richard Chase's book
Quest for Myth demonstrates that mankind has always
attempted to explain in some fashion the strange legends and stories that are a vital part of its heritage. The
main impetus, however, to modern myth study seems
to have been supplied by a group of British anthropologists, chiefly at Cambridge University, in the last part
of the nineteenth century. These men, the most prominent of whom are Sir E. B. Tylor, Andrew Lang, and
Sir James Frazer, seeing in the science of comparative
anthropology an opening into as yet unrealized methods of myth interpretation, proposed the theory that
myth represented primitive man's first attempts at philosophy, that behind the façade of supernaturalism and
magic could be discerned the workings of a mind that
relied on reason.

Outside the field of anthropology, a group of classical
scholars at Cambridge, using the comparative technique developed by Frazer, found that myth seemed to
be directly descended from primitive ritual. Thus Jane
Harrison, one of the foremost of the group, attempted
in her *Prolegomena to the Study of Greek Religion* and
later in *Themis* to show that myths were in reality the
spoken correlatives of forgotten rituals, for the most
part rituals involving some sort of propitiation of a
vegetation spirit. Following Miss Harrison's lead, Gil-
bert Murray[11] and F. M. Cornford[12] found myth and
ritual to be the basis of Greek drama; A. B. Cook examined Zeus;[13] Jessie L. Weston investigated the Grail

3

material;[14] Lord Raglan studied the incest taboo[15] and the figure of the mythical hero;[16] and Enid Welsford looked closely at the traditional character of the Fool.[17]

This ritual theory of myth thus adapted itself into a modern theory of literary criticism which takes as its point of departure the premise that any piece of literature can be reduced to a series of patterns derived from myth, which is itself derived from ritual. Thus, to cite only three of the many modern ritual studies, Constance Rourke in *American Humor* has succeeded in demonstrating that the characters and thematic patterns of the American myth—Uncle Sam, the Yankee trader—can be observed in representative works of American literature; Francis Fergusson in *The Idea of a Theatre* has reduced the structure of *Oedipus Rex* to what he calls a "tragic rhythm," "the ritual form" of the play, in order to use it as a touchstone for judging other tragic drama; and Richard Chase in works such as *Herman Melville* is interested in applying myth patterns, derived particularly from the Prometheus myth, to Melville and American literature.

The psychologists were quick to see that myth study held rewards for them also. In myth Freud saw manifestations of the same neurological states—particularly the Oedipus complex—which he had long observed in the minds of his patients. Freud was thus able to interpret in myth and in literature certain symbols, for the most part sexual, which he had encountered and diagnosed in the dreams of neurotic patients. Freud's disciple Carl G. Jung attacked the problem of myth even more directly. Jung conceived of myth as the least sophisticated and thus most accurate embodiment of a series of archetypes reflecting situations, attitudes, and symbols present in man's mind from the beginning of time and somehow passed along from generation to generation in the structure of the brain itself. The Jungian critic thus comes to see creative literature as a thin veil covering a core of unconsciously reasserted

4

myth archetypes. For example, Maud Bodkin, the most distinguished proponent of the method, connects the figure of Milton's Eve with Homer's goddesses, Proserpine, Delilah, Beatrice, Helen, Dido, Cleopatra, and Francesca di Rimini in order to show the varieties of the principal archetypes of woman as goddess, mother, destroyer.

Certain philosophers, among them Ernst Cassirer, Susanne Langer, and W. M. Urban, also saw great possibilities in the new myth study. Rejecting the theory held by Tylor and Frazer that the mythmaker is a child-like philosopher, Ernst Cassirer held in *Language and Myth* and in *The Philosophy of Symbolic Forms* that primitive man did not reason by laws of cause and effect, but instead tended simply to "image" by means of symbolic language his relations to the great world in which he found himself. Myth to these philosophers is thus preterlogical, the product of a mind that sees all experience as a whole, rather than as a series of logically classified parts. It is a symbolic language used by primitive man to define, symbolize, and thus render manageable his experience.

It is significant that the most influential theory of history in our time, that of Arnold J. Toynbee, is based on myth. In general, Toynbee sees in the quest-myth of the hero a formula that can be used to explain the rise and fall of civilizations in relation to their physical environments. Certainly Toynbee's formula of withdrawal and return offers enormous possibilities to the literary critic as well. Joseph Campbell has called the quest of the hero the "monomyth," the common denominator of all myth,[18] and Northrop Frye has framed a workable definition of comedy and tragedy in these terms.[19]

Although the results of the critics committed to these theories of myth have been valuable in that they have thrown new light on myth and on individual works of literature, it must be said that no one of them has as yet introduced a whole theory of myth which can be used

5

either in formulating a notion of what literature is or in explaining how it operates. The attention of these critics has been so drawn to the definition of myth itself that they have seldom had time to come to grips with the purely literary questions involved. They always ask what myth is, never how myth functions in literature.

The anthropologists, ritualists, psychologists, and philosophers thus become for the most part excellent myth hunters, but poor critics. In *Herman Melville*, Richard Chase's insistence on finding mythological referents for everything in Melville too often leads him away from the investigation of broad mythological patterns, a valuable literary strategy, into overly specific point-by-point applications of particular myths to Melville's text. Melville's Confidence Man becomes an absolute prototype of the traditional American figure of Brother Jonathan; the characters of *Pierre* are at one point completely identified with the churches of the Apocalypse; Ahab becomes a maimed and impotent Prometheus, Billy Budd a true and whole Prometheus. But Chase never raises any question of the particular function of these myths within the novels, of how they affect general structure or theme, or why they are used by Melville in the first place.

What is true of Chase is true generally of the other myth critics. Jessie L. Weston points out analogue after analogue of the Grail myth, forcing it finally into a ritualistic context, but to read *From Ritual to Romance* is to learn little, if anything, about Chrétien and Malory as writers. It is true that Maud Bodkin's *Studies of Type-Images in Poetry, Religion, and Philosophy* represents a valuable type of literary investigation in that by such a method the critic can come very quickly to the thematic center of a poem, but it is also true that all questions of structure, diction, and form are left behind in the mad rush for the central archetype. The sort of psychological criticism practiced by Freud himself is certainly revealing as a literary tour de force, but when

6

used extensively breaks down into meaningless biographical criticism.

It is apparent that all the defects of these possible ways of looking at myth in literature can be reduced to one fault. Myth is currently used as a sort of universal literary solvent; the unspoken assumption would seem to be "Let us reduce this poem, this novel, this play to its basic mythical, structural, ritual ingredients and there will then be an end to all critical problems." Such a point of view avoids the main literary problem raised by myth in literature, which, as I have said, is primarily a problem of function. To reduce a work of literature to its component ingredients and leave it there is a necessary methodology for the writer of source handbooks, but it is hardly a proper strategy for the critic who is committed to a study of the use made by the artist of these source materials. The works of nearly all critics concerned with myth in literature become too often studies of myth for the sake of myth rather than of literature.

What is obviously needed is a working definition of how myth functions in literature, of how the creative artist uses myth to convert the raw materials of chaotic experience into a finished artistic work that represents an ordered view of that experience. In attempting to frame such a definition, I approach my most difficult task. It will be apparent that much of what I have to say in arriving at my final statement is borrowed from others, particularly Cassirer. It will also be clear that the theory that I formulate here is in some ways related to the view of myth and poetry suggested by a number of modern critics, by Ransom, Eliot, and R. P. Warren among others. Yet the main value of the theory that I propose is that it fills a need in modern criticism in defining a general point of view toward the function of myth in literature which can be used to meet the problems raised by specific literary works.

We can, I think, assume that the Cambridge ritualists

7

have presented the most satisfactory theory of myth origin—that myth represents the spoken correlative to a forgotten ritual; as far as I know, it is the theory most generally acceptable. Yet it is necessary also that we take a stand on the sort of mentality required for such symbolic action. Many of the older critics and philosophers who dealt with myth, among them Kant, Tylor, and Frazer, maintained that primitive man was in essence a kind of crude scientist; that he reasoned as we reason, by cause and effect, and that he thought as we think, in perceptible logical patterns. Yet others, the most prominent of whom is Ernst Cassirer, maintain otherwise. "Myth," says Cassirer, "is not only far remote from this empirical reality; it is, in a sense, in flagrant contradiction to it. It seems to build up an entirely fantastic world. . . ."[20]

Of the two possibilities expressed here, the second seems more accurate to me. There are many elements in myth which point to a conception of primitive man as imagist rather than as conceptualist. In Frazer's description, the primitive is overintellectualized; the first thing that impresses a reader after reading a number of myths is that the associations made within the story become logical and explicable only when considered in retrospect; upon initial reading, their plots seem fantastic and their associations nonlogical and arbitrary. There is certainly no apparent system of theology or philosophy immediately present in such stories, as Tylor claimed there was.

Yet the fact remains that myth appears to have at least a modicum of logical structure; if this were not true, such compilations as Frazer's, in which myths are arranged and classified according to their similarity of pattern, would be impossible. We must, therefore, steer between a theory that regards myth as the product of a completely logical mentality and a theory that interprets myth as the purely emotional expression of a nonthinking savage mind.

8

If we retreat for a moment to the ritual acts from which myths come, we can see the beginnings of a solution. According to most commentators, there existed a time in the history of man when the "earth and every common sight" did in fact "seem / Appareled in celestial light." Thus Cassirer shows "the root of all Melanesian religion to be the concept of a 'supernatural power,' which permeates all things and events, and may be present now in objects, now in persons, yet is never bound exclusively to any single and individual subject or object as its host, but may be transmitted from place to place, from thing to thing, from person to person."[21] Primitive man thus regards the entire natural world in which he lives as intrinsically divine. Nature is itself a god, a gigantic potency usually called mana which infiltrates all human insights into the nature of things and affects every activity of everyday life. Ordinary daily living becomes in essence religious; every meal, every act of retiring and arising, every planting and harvesting begins to take upon itself set ritualistic patterns.

The next stage in man's religious development follows naturally. Certain acts become in time more intrinsically "holy" than other acts; almost by its very nature the act of sowing seed in the spring gives rise to the feelings of mingled hope and fear which we generally term "religious." At this point, then, appear the "momentary gods," "purely instantaneous, . . . fleeting, and emerging and vanishing content[s],"[22] reflecting a division of function within the mana; they are objectifications of man's attitudes toward the surprising and wonderful in his daily life, in which, we remember, everything was once surprising and wonderful. The rituals go on, but they now become limited to special areas of human endeavor and in doing so take on a special importance and a more elaborate ceremonial.

The history of religious thought passes on into various stages of objectification in which the religious attitude becomes expressed in terms of more and more

9

specialized and personalized beings. But the myth-making period would seem to me to precede this strict sort of anthropomorphism and to reside in the earlier days when the new gods had not yet become wholly distinct from the great mana that pervaded everything, when a sudden insight into nature revealed mysteries of overpowering force.

The problem for man, then, was to seize on and sustain the emotions of those momentary flashes of insight, to record them somehow for his future use in order to propitiate the "force" if it were evil, or to praise it if it were kindly. The medium was at hand—language; yet what sort of language this primitive man had at his disposal needs separate attention.

At this time, we must hypostatize a semihistorical period when all language was unified in function, when there was no difference between a man's normal speech and the language of poetry and ritual. This unification of language, like the unification of the religious attitude, can be said to be primarily a result of the primitive man's basic world view that regarded nature as a whole and undivided complex, not as yet separated into the logical divisions—man and nature, subjective and objective—upon which more sophisticated men base their daily actions. Henri Frankfort states that "any phenomenon may at any time face [primitive man], not as 'It,' but as 'Thou.' . . . 'Thou' is not contemplated with intellectual detachment; it is experienced as life confronting life. . . ."[23] In short, to this primitive point of view, there could be no distinction between fairy tale and scientific statement. Language was as yet undifferentiated by function into logical statement and intuitive statement. Man had only one mode of thought and language—that which Henri Frankfort calls the speculative, an "intuitive, an almost visionary, mode of apprehension" which "attempts to *underpin* the chaos of experience so that it may reveal the features of a structure—order, coherence, and meaning."[24]

10

This last phrase is of the greatest importance. In using language to formulate the fleeting impressions of momentary gods, man was attempting to bring order out of chaos, to reveal within the universe some sort of stability, some sort of patterned meaning by which he could live and in terms of which he could manipulate the nature that surrounded him. The "ultimate end [of myth] is not wishful distortion of the world, but serious envisagement of its fundamental truths; moral orientation, not escape. . . ."[25] Myth, then, comes out of this desire for order, manifesting itself in rituals of appeasement, in a confusion of things seen and unseen, and expressing itself by means of a preterlogical language.

Yet in the making and ritualistic use of myth, one more attribute exhibits itself. Having recorded and conserved his religious sense impressions by means of language in terms of myth, primitive man is able to manipulate symbolically the sacred objects by means of the myths that he has constructed as their symbols. "The primitive," says Henri Frankfort, "uses symbols as much as we do; but he can no more conceive them as signifying, yet separate from the gods or powers than he can consider a relationship established in his mind—such as resemblance—as connecting, and yet separate from, the objects compared. Hence there is coalescence of the symbol and what it signifies, as there is coalescence of two objects compared so that one may stand for the other. . . . For us there is an essential difference between an act and a ritual or symbolic performance. But this distinction was meaningless to the ancients."[26] Myth in its earliest forms clearly exhibits this confusion of symbol and object which is typical of the primitive, mythmaking mentality.

We may now return to answer our original question. It can be said that myth partakes of both the emotional and the rational. It is emotional in that it represents the activity of a preterlogical mode of thought which does not depend upon reason and logic; it is ordered and meaningful in that it is an attempt to order an existence and an experience naturally chaotic. This is the reason, as I see it, that myth strikes the modern reader as both a worthless primitive curiosity and, at the same time, a valid commentary upon its author's experience. Myth orders experience, but in terms that are essentially alien to our own. It is a commentary on the problems of life, but a commentary in a language that we can no longer read. Thus myth itself can be said to possess two qualities upon which a theory of purely literary criticism may reasonably be based: (1) it, like perhaps all literature, is an attempt to bring order out of the chaos of experience; and (2) like most poetry, it conducts its affairs by means of symbolic language that serves to block and counteract the direct movement and logical progression of the poem.

I would postulate at this point the existence of a special sort of creative mentality, a mentality which, like that of the primitive, either cannot or will not see that the poetic symbol and the reality that that symbol reflects possess any essential difference in kind. We have seen that myth itself reflects such a point of view, and it is my point here that this same particular sort of attitude toward symbolic action may be observed in modern artists as well. It is true, of course, that the primitive creates myth by means of a world view that by its very nature sees the "World in a Grain of Sand / And a Heaven in a Wild Flower"; the modern poet can acquire such a view only through conscious effort. Such a point of view depends, in both cases, on a reconciliation of opposites, on a desire and ability, whether natural or consciously intended, to unite, and by uniting to order, disparate items of nature and experience.

The exact method by which the human mind accomplishes this feat has never been thoroughly explained; perhaps a complete explanation of the process is impossible. Coleridge, of all the critics, attacks the problem most directly and with the best results. Generally, Coleridge felt that poetic unity could only be revealed as a synthesis of polar opposites, in a fusion of likeness and unlikeness, sameness and difference, universality and particularity. These opposites, however, cannot reconcile themselves. There is always present, in Coleridge's scheme, a third element, a copula, capable of uniting these disparate items into a single poetic substance, partaking of the qualities of both its ingredients, but essentially different from either. In poetry, the Reason, that faculty of the mind which deals with ordered abstraction, and the Understanding, the faculty devoted to the organization of material experience, are combined by the Imagination, which joins these faculties into a poetic attitude capable of fusing material image (the product of the Understanding) with abstract idea (the product of the Reason) into poetry, which is both image and idea. What Coleridge is describing here is the process whereby the poetic mind comes to identify symbol and object. Yet Coleridge himself would seem to believe that this sort of analysis necessarily follows the act that it describes, that the actual process is itself a reconciliation of Intuition and the poet's will to unify and create.[27] Seen in these terms, the difference between ancient primitive and modern poet becomes mainly one of simple intent. The primitive performs these acts of unification automatically; the poet wills that the process be initiated; in both cases, the psychology involved is the same. This reconciliation would seem to be demonstrable, moreover, in an examination of the relationship of symbol and object within the poem.

The relationship of symbol and object within the poem is, of course, a highly complex problem and one that I cannot pretend to settle. On the other hand, although there certainly exist relationships of varying degrees of complexity between the two, the extremes of this relative scale can be pointed out and examined. Let me introduce at this point two metaphorical passages in demonstration, the first from Donne, the second from Pope:

> Whilst my physicians by their love are grown
> Cosmographers, and I their map, who lie
> Flat on this bed, that by them may be shown
> That this is my Southwest discovery
> *Per fretum febris,* by these straits to die,
>
> I joy that in these straits I see my West;
> For though their currents yield return to none,
> What shall my West hurt me? As West and East
> In all flat maps (and I am one) are one,
> So death doth touch the resurrection.
>   ("Hymn to God, My God, in My Sickness")
>
> Fir'd at first sight with what the Muse imparts,
> In fearless youth we tempt the heights of Arts,
> While from the bounded level of our mind,
> Short views we take, nor see the lengths behind;
> But, more advanc'd, behold with strange surprise,
> New distant scenes of endless science rise!
> So pleas'd at first the tow'ring Alps we try,
> Mount o'er the vales, and seem to tread the sky,
> Th' eternal snows appear already past,
> And the first clouds and mountains seem the last;
> But, those attain'd, we tremble to survey
> The growing labours of the lengthen'd way,
> Th' increasing prospect tires our wand'ring eyes,
> Hills peep o'er hills, and Alps on Alps arise.
>   ("Essay on Criticism")

The first selection represents a relationship, sometimes called "sacramental," between the tenor and the vehicle of the metaphor. The distinguishing quality of the symbol-object relationship within the passage is that an actual substitution takes place. The poet begins by stating the terms he is going to develop; his attendant physicians are mapmakers and his prostrate body the

14

map. Having made this initial statement of the basic identification concerned, the poet then proceeds with the argument of the poem. Yet here we cannot but be struck by a startling fact. The tenor of the poem is the approaching death of the poet's body and subsequent salvation of his soul. Yet the poet only once within the confines of the metaphor (*"per fretum febris"*) discusses the tenor of the metaphor directly in its own terms once he has left it. The dialectic of the passage proceeds almost entirely in terms of the vehicle, the geographers and the map. Instead of illnesses and death and resurrection directly, we have talk of straits and currents and East and West, until the very end of the passage, when, having given his proof in terms of the vehicle, the poet states his conclusion ("So death doth touch the resurrection") in terms of the tenor.

The second poet proceeds, it seems to me, by means of a different strategy. We have first a recital of the tenor, a complete account of the young critic's difficulties. Then, having explained the referent thoroughly, we are given *as illustration* a metaphor describing the young critic's difficulties in terms of a traveler's struggle to climb the Alps. Thus this relationship, which I call "illustrative," never mixes its terms. The dialectic of the poem goes step by step in terms of its tenor and interrupts this logical progression at times to illustrate metaphorically what has already been said.

The sacramental point of view manifests itself, I think, in the first of these poetic strategies, but not in the second. In the first selection, the poet succeeds in making a complete identification of both parts of his metaphor within the context of the poem. The argument of the poem may thus proceed quite naturally in terms of the vehicle of the metaphor as well as in terms of its tenor. The translation of vehicle and tenor is in essence representative of the same identification of symbol and object which we have already remarked on as one of the distinguishing characteristics of myth, and the presence of such a poetic method seems to me to demonstrate the workings of the mythic and sacramental point of view.

A similar demonstration can, of course, be made in religious ritual. The doctrine of the Real Presence held by the more conservative communions of the Church—Roman, Anglican, and Lutheran—defines just such a relationship. In asserting that Christ is truly and substantially present on the altar, these churches are asserting that symbol and object, sign and grace are in fact so inextricably mixed that the grace cannot be transmitted except in terms of its sacramental symbol, the material sign of the Sacrament. Moreover, it is apparent in the Eucharistic rituals of all three communions that, as in the first selection of poetry quoted above, the progress of the ceremony following the identification of symbol and object in the Consecration is conducted entirely in terms of the Body and Blood. Thus physical symbol and metaphysical object become fused into a single sacramental object that contains within itself both symbol and object and may express itself in either set of terms.

So far I have suggested the sort of sacramental mentality responsible for the creation of myth, and I have indicated a possible way of detecting such a mentality in works of art. This sacramental point of view in the creative artist is, of course, closely akin to the speculative, intuitive, preterlogical thought seen in myth creation. In both cases, this fusion is demonstrable by an analysis of the terms of the comparison. The sort of symbolic action produced by this sacramental point of view results in the particular sort of intertranslation of vehicle and tenor commonly noted in the poetry of Donne, Coleridge, Hopkins, and Eliot. It can thus be separated from the illustrative metaphorical structure of Pope and from the purely allegorical method of Dryden's *The Hind and the Panther.*

By saying that the sacramentalist-mythmaker-poet can live in two worlds, in both halves of a metaphor, simultaneously, we have advanced a little nearer to an answer to the problem of the function of myth in literature. Both illustrations I have used involve the use of symbols of the poets' own making. The comparison of body and map was created by Donne especially for use in this poem; the same is true of Pope's comparison of the young critic with the mountain climber. Compare for a moment those passages with the following lines:

> The nightingales are singing near
> The Convent of the Sacred Heart,
>
> And sang within the bloody wood
> When Agamemnon cried aloud,
> And let their liquid siftings fall
> To stain the stiff dishonoured shroud.

(T. S. Eliot, "Sweeney among the Nightingales")
The sacramental point of view is certainly present in these lines; the poet shifts, within the poem, from a cheap modern tavern into the myth world of Philomel and Agamemnon and back again to Sweeney's "stiff dishonoured shroud." In fact, the two scenes, in the eyes of the poet, are coexistent in time and space. Yet here the symbols used by the poet are not of his own making; the initial connection between Sweeney and Agamemnon certainly exists only within the mind of Eliot, but Philomel and Agamemnon as mythical figures bring to the poem a great body of connotative material for which, unlike Donne with his map, Eliot bears no responsibility. Again:

> I dream of a Ledaean body, bent
> Above a sinking fire . . .

(William Butler Yeats, "Among School Children")
The same method is seen in operation here. By the symbolical use of the adjective "Ledaean" the poet is able to introduce into the poem the natural emotional suggestions inherent in the myth of Leda and the Swan. The poet is responsible only for the initial connection that the symbol makes; the mythic referents themselves

17

then begin to act within the poem on their own inherent terms.

Myth in the creative art of the sacramentalist poet becomes then a special sort of symbol at once more complex and more meaningful than the symbol of the poet's own making. Myth, when used as symbol, brings with it the complexity of its own milieu, which becomes free to operate on its own terms within the poem. The poet can thus use a metaphorical reference to myth, as William Butler Yeats does in the example above, in order to call forth by implication the whole substance and meaning of that myth. Myth thus functions as a whole symbol, already ordered and complete in itself, which the poet may use as a poetic referent in order to facilitate the ordering of his particular experience and point of view within the poem.

It is apparent, moreover, that this symbolical use of myth by the sacramentalist poet depends to a large degree upon an Act of Faith, a "willing suspension of disbelief which constitutes poetic faith," on the part of the reader as well as of the poet. The reader must be willing to accept temporarily the terms of the comparison that the poet has constructed. And because myth when used as symbol endows the poem with a more complex metaphorical structure than does the usual symbol, the reader is drawn further and further into the initial identification of symbol and object made by the poet. Thus by the use of myth as symbol the poet not only increases the richness and fullness of his own ordering of experience, but the reader as well comes to understand the poet's statement more thoroughly, since he need not rely wholly upon the poet's arbitrary metaphorical pattern but can bring to the poem and exploit in his reading of it the general knowledge of the myth referent which he already possesses. Thus, the reader will presumably see the full connection that Yeats intends him to see between Leda and the young Maud Gonne in "Among School Children," by applying what he already knows about the myth of Leda. The poet and the reader are therefore able to call upon a large general stock of already ordered and meaningful knowledge—the one in arranging and condensing his thought into the strict forms of poetic composition, the other in recreating in his own mind the fullness of the poetic expression.

Myth in literature thus functions as a great stockpile of common imagery on which the poet may draw at any time in order to condense and reorder his ideas into the shapes required by formal literature. Moreover, in using myth as sacramental rather than as illustrative metaphor, the poet can unify the disordered world he sees around him with the ordered world represented by myth by imposing that order upon the chaotic structure of his own experience. Thus it is that we find such modern poets as Yeats, Auden, and Eliot retreating temporarily into a world of myth in order to find an order they can impose upon their own disordered world. Eliot's comment on the use of myth in *Ulysses* is perhaps a perfect expression of this point of view; myth, says Eliot, is "a way of controlling, of ordering, of giving a shape and a significance to the immense panorama of futility and anarchy which is contemporary history."[28] In short, the myth brings stature, order, and meaning to the modern writer's attempts to order the chaotic world of his own time.

2

The Arthurian Myth

IF MYTH FUNCTIONS in literary art as an ordering symbol,
complete and meaningful within itself, which the literary artist can use sacramentally in order to impose that
mythical order upon the statement of his own experience, then the function of myth in literature would seem
to be at least partly accounted for. It may be objected,
of course, that any symbol, not just that derived from
myth, performs this same function. However, these ordinary symbols of the poet's own making cannot approach the connotative wealth of the myth symbol since
(1) they depend to a large extent on individual impressions and opinions of the referent involved rather than
on a commonly shared body of prejudged information,
and (2) these nonmythical symbols seldom, if ever,
carry with them the connotative weight of a fully expressed and highly developed situation, the motives and
character relations of which are already ordered and
complete. In using a nonmythical symbol, then, the
poet must in a sense interpret his symbols as he goes
along; if he uses a metaphorical reference to myth, this
task is accomplished for him because the mythical referent carries with it its own prejudged interpretation.

In the following chapters, I shall deal with the Arthurian myth as it appears in the works of three modern
British writers; I shall treat this myth, moreover, as a
particular point of reference by which to ascertain the

functional use of myth in the works of each of them. Yet even at the outset a perplexing question intrudes: Can what is generally called the Arthurian "legend" be legitimately used as a touchstone in investigating the use of "myth"? Some discussion at this point of the differences between legend and myth will not only help to characterize the development of the Arthurian story, but will also serve to illuminate the point of view and attitude from which Williams, Lewis, and Eliot view their Arthurian materials.

The usual distinction between the two terms, made some time ago by Bethe, is that "myth, legend, and fairytale differ from one another in origin and purpose. Myth is primitive philosophy, the simplest presentational . . . form of thought, a series of attempts to understand the world, to explain life and death, fate and nature, gods and cults. Legend is primitive history, naïvely formulated in terms of love and hate, unconsciously transformed and simplified. But fairytale has sprung from, and serves, no motive but entertainment."[1] In discussing this distinction, Susanne Langer designates as the distinctive mark of legend the presence of the "culture-hero" whose attributes she lists:

He is half god, half giant-killer. Like the latter, he is often a Youngest Son, the only clever one among his stupid brothers. He is born of high parentage, but kidnapped, or exposed and rescued, or magically enslaved, in his infancy. Unlike the dream-subject of fairytale, however, his deeds only begin with his escape from thralldom; they go on to benefit mankind. He gives men fire, territory, game, teaches them agriculture, ship-building, perhaps even language; he "makes" the land, finds the sun (in a cave, in an egg, or in a foreign country), and sets it in the sky, and controls wind and rain.[2]

Legend can thus be said to fulfill the same function in the evolution of literary form as did the creation of the objectified Homeric gods in the history of religion. Legend does not exhibit a pure sacramentalism; there is no fusion, no real identification of symbol and object, but a situation in which the hero, on whose actions legendary art focuses, and other characters can accurately be said to represent or illustrate general attributes. In the progress of myth to fiction can be seen one stage of the movement from the sacramental to the illustrative metaphorical technique.

Certainly then from one point of view the great body of Arthurian material can technically be called legendary. We have in Arthur what appears to be a "culture-hero" whose exploits become the principal subject of the story. In the first full account of the tale, that of Geoffrey of Monmouth, and throughout what is called the "chronicle tradition" of Wace and Layamon, the legendary cast of the story is seemingly clear. One brilliant military exploit follows another; Arthur moves from triumph to triumph in the grand manner. There is no general unifying theme in these early versions of the story; they are chronicles, nonthematic histories, pure listings of events, which never allow their straightforward accounts of physical action to become complicated by irrelevant questions of structure or theme. Yet even though the Arthurian story as it appears in the chronicle tradition is more nearly a true legend in Mrs. Langer's terms than it ever is afterward, it is even here more nearly a nonthematic history than a "legend." To refer for a moment to Mrs. Langer's statement, it will be seen that Arthur, although superficially a legendary culture-hero, in fact lacks the prime characteristics of the type. It is true, of course, that the events surrounding Arthur's conception are semimagical. But he cannot be said to have been "kidnapped" in youth or to be the bearer of cultural gifts—"fire, territory, game, . . . agriculture, . . . shipbuilding, . . . language"—nor can he be said to represent or illustrate any abstract virtue or concept; he is primarily a heightened chivalric hero and if he represents anything at all, it is as J. D. Bruce says, "a great medieval monarch."[3] The early chroniclers did not, I am certain, see Arthur as a cultural hero nor did they envisage him in terms of the ideal pattern of heroic behavior.[4] The last movement of the withdrawal-return cycle, that in which the hero returns with his gifts, is never accomplished since Arthur never makes use of the lessons learned in a withdrawal from the world and, as Toynbee points out, this last movement of the pattern, the hero's return to his own country, is essential.[5]

What I am saying—that the Arthur of the early chronicles is neither a mythical nor a legendary hero— is perhaps obvious without demonstration, but I am eager for the reader to see that the Arthurian story does not begin as legendary history, but rather as unmotivated folk history. It is apparent, moreover, that in the later courtly and religious tradition, the story never assumes the qualities of a legend, but instead comes more and more to resemble what we generally mean by the word "myth." In the reworkings of the story by the French romancers, principally Marie de France, Chrétien de Troyes, and the author (or authors) of the great thirteenth-century Vulgate Prose Cycle, two highly developed literary traditions become attached to the hitherto themeless story of the chroniclers—courtly love and Christian mysticism—traditions that were in fact violently opposed. Wherever or for whatever reasons the cult of courtly love originated, it was already a highly developed concept when it became connected with the Arthurian story. The Grail story, on the other hand, is first seen in connection with the Arthurian material in Chrétien's *Conte del Graal*, but it appears in that first version almost full blown. My primary point concerning the addition of these concepts to the Arthurian story as it appears in the romancers is this: the themes of courtly love and the Holy Grail serve to start a chain of development in the Arthurian story which results in giving a theme to the chronicle story. In their first appearances these two additions are seen as affecting only individual segments of the story; for example, courtly love is first seen in such isolated adventures as Chrétien's *Knight of the Cart* and the Grail in Chrétien's *Conte del Graal,* both of which are primarily adventures of single knights who bear, at least in Chrétien, only a very loose connection with the whole society of the Round Table. However, in the thirteenth-century Vulgate Cycle to some degree, and more clearly in Malory's *Morte Darthur,* the unifying influence of the two themes is visible; the theme of courtly love as seen in Lancelot and Guinevere, Tristram and Iseult pervades the story from beginning to end and there are hints in Malory that the "passage of the Grail destroyed the kingdom."[6] The romancers would seem to have endowed what was essentially a medieval chronicle of events with a central structure based on the reiteration of these two guiding concepts of love and religion, and with a central theme based on their opposition within the story. It is perhaps indicative of this movement toward thematic unity that Arthur himself, the original hero of the story, fades more and more into the background as it becomes increasingly apparent that he cannot be used in developing these major themes.

Return for a moment to Bethe's definitions of myth, legend, and fairy tale. If we apply this distinction to the Arthurian story as it exists in its most complete medieval version, that of Malory, it becomes clear that the story may be classified either as legend or as myth, depending on the point of view of the observer. On one level, the story can be considered as legend; its major purpose is the mere historical description of the rise and fall of a kingdom, its all-important character relationships somewhat "naïvely formulated in terms of love and hate." On another level, however, the story may be legitimately considered as myth; its major purpose is not historical description, but metaphysical speculation on the meaning of history, its character relationships indicative not merely of the temporal clash of purely human emotions, but of human conflicts as they exist in relation to the whole universe in which they function. According to this mythical point of view, the Arthurian story is concerned only incidentally with man in his earthly dealings; its true subject is the relationship of God and man, its true purpose an attempt "to understand the world, to explain life and death, fate and nature."

Thus it is natural that a reader looking at the story in terms of parts, of isolated quests and adventures, will see the material as legend, as accounts of the loves and knightly deeds of a group of individual heroes. On the other hand, however, a reader who sees the story in terms of a whole structure will see the material as myth, as the working out in literary terms of a metaphysical theme. I should like to avoid, if possible, a personal choice between the two interpretations. However, the three writers with whom I am dealing in this study have, I believe, elected to look upon and use the Arthurian story as myth rather than as legend in their writings. Each of them is primarily involved with the story seen as a whole in that each of them devotes his principal attention to the Grail material, which from the second of these points of view is almost certain to be the focusing point of the story. Even T. S. Eliot, who in *The Waste Land* uses the Grail material only in the form in which it appears in Chrétien, considers the Grail episode as a microcosm of the principal theme of the whole story, envisioned by him as the clash of religious fertility and secular sterility. Moreover, in using the Arthurian story essentially as an ordering metaphor, these modern writers have demonstrated that its central theme is essentially coherent and that its parts may be used symbolically to suggest the ordered and unified whole myth from which they were taken. It is noteworthy also that there would seem to be no difference of opinion among these three men as to what constitutes the basic theme of the story; as it is used by each of them, the Arthurian myth involves principally the failure of a would-be perfect secular civilization to preserve itself by an alliance with the religious principles symbolized by the Grail. The fact, then, that each of these modern writers is able to use the Arthurian story as a sacramental and ordering symbol that has a discernible central theme would seem to indicate that these writers view the Arthurian materials as myth rather than as legend.

Since the three writers with whom I am to deal place their main emphases on the Grail section of the Arthurian myth, a summary of the development of that story would be appropriate here. The Grail first appears in Chrétien de Troyes's *Conte del Graal,* which was written during the last quarter of the twelfth century. According to one tradition, Chrétien died during its composition. At any rate, the poem is unfinished and its fragmentary form tempted other writers of the time to continue the adventure of Perceval, Chrétien's Grail knight. The most famous of these continuators is Robert de Boron, who in *Joseph* supplied the early history of the Grail itself. According to Robert (and we must remember here that Robert's history followed and was probably inspired by Chrétien's poem), Joseph of Arimathea immediately after the Crucifixion received from Pilate the cup that was used by Christ at the Last Supper. In the process of removing the Body from the Cross this same cup was used to catch the Blood that flowed from the newly opened wounds. The cup was then buried in Joseph's house. Joseph was a short time later imprisoned, but here Christ appeared to him in a vision, gave him the cup as a symbol of His trust, and commanded him to keep it. Joseph was later released by Vespasian and went into exile, presumably into England, with his followers. After many adventures, the Grail was passed on to Bron, Joseph's brother-in-law, who acquired the title of the "Rich Fisher."

Chrétien's *Conte del Graal,* which precedes Robert's *Joseph,* deals with the adventures of a young man named Perceval, who, upon seeing a group of Arthur's knights, is inspired to become a knight. Leaving his grief-stricken mother, he makes his way to Arthur's court. Setting out in quest of a Red Knight, he encounters an old knight named Gournemant who instructs him in knighthood; among other pieces of advice, Gournemant warns him against asking questions. On his way homeward, however, Perceval encounters Gournemant's niece Blanchefleur, whose castle is besieged by the forces of King Clamadeus. Perceval, after spending the night with Blanchefleur, agrees to defend her and succeeds in killing Clamadeus. At this point in the story begins the Grail episode proper. Perceval, bound again for home, comes upon two men fishing in a boat who give him directions to a nearby castle. Upon entering the castle, he finds himself in a great hall where he sees an old man sleeping upon a couch and some four hundred of his attendants sleeping about him. A squire enters and presents Perceval with a sword; shortly thereafter, another squire enters carrying a lance that bleeds at its point. Perceval considers inquiring about the meaning of the strange performance, but remembering Gournemant's advice keeps silent. Two more squires enter, carrying ten-branched candelabra; with them is a young girl carrying a vessel (*graal*) which lights the room. Following her is another maiden carrying a silver plate. Here and during the meal that follows, Perceval again restrains his natural desire to question the meaning of the proceedings. Perceval retires and upon arising the following morning finds the castle deserted. After leaving the castle, he comes upon a maiden, who tells him that the fisherman who directed him to the castle and the old man on the couch were in fact the same person—the Fisher King who had been wounded in the thighs by a spear thrust. She further informs him that had he asked the meaning of what he had seen, the wounded king would have been healed and a great good would have resulted. The poem goes on to other adventures of Perceval and Gawain and we hear no more of the Fisher King, although Perceval is told later that his failure at the Grail Castle was a result of his having killed his mother through callousness.

At the beginning of the *Conte del Graal*, Chrétien states that this "best tale" was taken from a book given to him by Count Philip d'Alsace and from this statement stems most of the controversy that rages over the origins of the story; for how much, ask the critics, of the Grail material was Chrétien responsible, and what was the character of the lost book he received from his patron? As J. D. Bruce points out, Chrétien generally treats his source materials very freely; he seldom merely versifies a "story that lay before him."[7] But even Bruce, who is generally willing to allow Chrétien the utmost freedom in handling his sources, goes on to say that "the book which Chrétien refers to . . . gave him the conception of the Grail. . . ."[8] If we grant to Chrétien, therefore, the credit for the development of the Grail characters, for the quest motif, and for the general connection with the Arthurian world, the question narrows down to the problem of the origin of the Grail itself. There are, at present, three opposed theories of origin: (1) that the Grail was originally a part of the Celtic folklore tradition, (2) that it sprang originally from a pagan vegetation ritual, and (3) that it was from the beginning a part of the Christian legend.

The theory of Celtic origin has been advanced mainly by Alfred Nutt,[9] A. C. L. Brown,[10] and R. S. Loomis.[11] Generally these scholars maintain that the Grail originated in Celtic food-supplying vessels; the Irish cauldron of Dagda, which magically supplied warriors with unending quantities of food, and the Welsh cauldron of Bran, which brought the dead to life, have been suggested as possible sources. Professor Brown, in a rather complex theory, has decided that in the mythical wars of the Irish good and bad fairies may be found the "basis from which grew the battles of King Arthur and his knights against outlandish foes in the romances,"[12] since these battles were fought over the magic talismans of Tuatha Dé—the spear, sword, stone, and *criol*—the last of which Brown identifies as the source of the Grail. R. S. Loomis, who also makes claims for a Celtic folklore Arthurian tradition, has been able to trace most of the names of Chrétien's Grail characters back to their Celtic beginnings. Another Celticist, Albert Pauphilet, has suggested that the episode of the Grail question alone is central to the story in Chrétien and that the talismans of the Grail, the spear and the processions, were added simply to give the story color.[13] In short, these Celticists, all of whom adhere to the doctrine that the whole body of Arthurian lore stems from Celtic beginnings to which it may be traced, hold that the Grail as well as the other miraculous objects in the Grail procession may be seen as talismans of Celtic folklore.

The second major theory of the origin of the Grail is that advanced by the ritualists, whose most articulate spokesmen are Jessie L. Weston[14] and W. A. Nitze.[15] Nitze argues that the Grail myth is based on a ritual celebration of a vegetative deity. The Fisher King is to Nitze "the symbol of the creative, fructifying force in nature, specifically associated with water . . . ,"[16] and the Grail knight is the initiate who is attempting to qualify for the service of the Grail; on his success depends the success of the harvest. The Grail itself represents a talisman, a "Holy Box" that was used in the early mysteries. Miss Weston's theory is for the most part identical with Nitze's except that whereas Nitze explains the lost ritual of the Grail cult by comparing it with partly known Eleusinian mysteries, Miss Weston takes as a point of departure the Adonis rites. Thus, the Fisher King becomes a type of the Slain God. Miss Weston, however, sometimes leaves the safe company of Sir James Frazer and slips across the line into Freudianism. The Fisher King's wound becomes a symbolic castration; the lance and cup, male and female phallic symbols; the legend as a whole, a record of the "search into the secret mystery of life . . . the record of an initiation *manqué*."[17]

The last of the three major theories of the origin of the Grail holds that the entire Grail myth is from the beginning a part of the Christian tradition.[18] The defenders of the theory of Christian origin generally claim that the original of the Grail procession is to be found in the ritual of the Byzantine Mass, in which the chalice and paten, along with a lance-like knife used to cut the Bread, are carried in procession. It is also maintained that the Fisher King may himself represent Christ who was in His own time symbolized by a fish. Urban T. Holmes and Sister M. Amelia Klenke have recently suggested an important modification of the theory of Christian origin.[19] Taking as a point of departure the fact that the medieval literary man used a story (*matière*) to carry a theme (*sens*) that could be interpreted on various levels of meaning, this theory suggests that the Grail castle is a "symbolical representation of the Temple of Solomon in Jerusalem, colored with some of the trappings of medieval feudalism. The Grail, the lance, the blood, the silver plate were the vessel of manna, Aaron's rod . . . , the blood of sacrifice made by the High Priest, and the tablet of the Law."[20] The Grail story becomes "the conversion of the Jewish Temple to Christianity,"[21] and the *Conte del Graal* a Christian allegory of conversion drawn from Chrétien's own experience.

It should be clear in thus reviewing these theories of the origin of the Grail that no one of them, as the situation now stands, can explain adequately all the elements of the Grail story as it appears in Chrétien's basic text. On the other hand, in spite of these disagreements among critics, we can be sure of at least one fact, that the Grail, whatever its origins, first attracts the serious consideration of the medieval literary world as a Christian story. Certainly Robert de Boron, the first interpreter of Chrétien's story (which, we remember, never explains the Grail symbols in any terms) saw the Grail as a Christian symbol and was inspired to write a long history of the Grail as a part of the Christian tradition; we can be relatively sure that Robert's contemporaries saw the Grail from the same point of view, and I should think it also possible to maintain that Chrétien must have known that his story would be taken as Christian allegory when he wrote it. The simplest explanation, then, is that this interpretation is what Chrétien intended, that his *matière* is a quest story centering in a mysterious castle and that his intended *sens* is the effect of the rejection of Christianity on a young and sinful knight. And it is this interpretation, in spite of the opposing critics, which has affected the literary tradition; there is, as far as I know, no great literary work treating the Grail which does not interpret it as a purely Christian symbol. Thus, we can make the generalization that if a modern writer uses the Grail myth as the sort of traditional, metaphorical symbol I have described, he is committed from the outset to a Christian interpretation of the symbol.

I have made so far in this chapter four major points concerning the relationship between the writers with whom I am to deal and the Arthurian myth: (1) that each of them looks at the Arthurian material as a whole structure rather than as a series of parts, as myth rather than as legend, (2) that each abstracts from that whole a single and generally agreed upon theme, (3) that this theme centers on the episode of the Grail quest, and (4) that these writers are committed by the literary tradition of the Grail (as well as by their own inclinations) to treat it as a purely Christian symbol. Each of the writers thus interprets the whole Arthurian myth as the exposition of a single religious theme—the failure of secularism in society.

But the center of the story, from another point of view, may not lie in the Grail material at all. Certainly, for one thing, the Grail episode comes late into the whole body of the tradition; it cannot be said to be a part of the main stream of Arthurian tradition until its inclusion in the thirteenth-century Vulgate Cycle. Even here, the Grail episode is hardly unified with the rest of the Arthurian adventures; the relationship of Lancelot and Guinevere would seem closer to being a central theme. The Grail section in the Vulgate Cycle seems almost a theological tract, a treatise on salvation, an Arthurian story in name only. It is only with Malory that the Grail material becomes integrated with the whole story.

Malory's great contribution to Arthurian literature as a whole is that he saw and to some degree exploited the possibilities for unity inherent, though disguised, in the Vulgate Cycle, his principal source. Certainly this is true of the Grail episode. Malory is careful to connect the Grail story, which constitutes the sixth large section of the *Morte Darthur,* with the whole *Morte Darthur.*[22] But this is not to say that the Grail story necessarily becomes the center of the story for Malory. Only from a certain point of view, that which regards the Arthurian story as myth rather than as legend, is the Grail material at the thematic center of Malory's version of the story. Malory's book may be interpreted to show that internal strife, occasioned for the most part by Lancelot's affair with the Queen, brings about the fall of the kingdom. To defend for a moment this interpretation, it is certainly true that from the very beginning Malory places a strong emphasis upon the importance of the character of Lancelot by extending his role in the action far beyond those duties assigned him in his sources.[23] Certainly, also, it is true that Malory from the beginning provides a motivation for the final catastrophe by pointing out quite clearly the steps in the developing love of Lancelot and Guinevere. From this point of view, then, the central conflict in Malory is between chivalric duty and romantic love, and the Grail material can only be considered as a quest in a long series of quests.

I think, moreover, that this almost completely secularized interpretation of the Arthurian story is that which comes down through the centuries as the accepted Arthurian tradition. In this tradition, the Grail quest quite naturally assumes a position of secondary importance. Certainly this attitude is found in the greatest modern version of the story, Tennyson's "The Holy Grail," one of the poems in *The Idylls of the King*. In the scene, taken from Malory, in which Arthur mourns the departure of the Grail knights, Tennyson has Arthur express the major attitude and theme of the poem:

> Then when he asked us, knight by knight, if any
> Had seen it [the Grail], all their answers were as
> one:
> 'Nay, lord, and therefore have we sworn our vows.'
> 'Lo, now,' said Arthur, 'have ye seen a cloud?
> What go ye into the wilderness to see?'

This tone of skepticism is repeated throughout the scene:

> 'Ah, Galahad, Galahad,' said the King, 'for such
> As thou art the vision, not for these.
> . . . and ye [the other knights],
> What are ye? Galahads?—no, nor Percivales'—
> . . .
> But one hath seen, and all the blind will see.
> Go, since your vows are sacred, being made.
> Yet—for ye know the cries of all my realm
> Pass through this hall—how often, O my knights,
> Your places being vacant at my side,
> This chance of noble deeds will come and go
> Unchallenged, while ye follow wandering fires
> Lost in the quagmire! Many of you, yea most,
> Return no more.'

Thus, in Tennyson's version, the quest of the Grail becomes one of the factors contributing to the downfall of the kingdom, but only because it is attempted by all of the knights, worthy and unworthy alike. It would seem that Tennyson is here rejecting the mystical Grail tradition entirely in saying that the Round Table would be far better off if the knights would refrain from attempting such an obviously chimerical task, if they would instead attend to the ordinary daily tasks of helping those in difficulty. Certainly, Tennyson thinks that the Grail is only for the devout few and that the great majority of knights are following a mistaken zeal and vision that are essentially alien to the expressed aims of chivalry. I think it is possible to say, therefore, that the Grail reaches a position in Tennyson almost wholly opposite in meaning and emphasis from that which it had held in the work of Chrétien. The progress of the Grail would seem then to originate in Chrétien's Christian mysticism, then to move, still retaining its devoutly religious tone, into the context of the Arthurian story in the French *Queste*. From there, the story progresses into a slightly more secularized version in Malory, and finally into a position where it represents a wrong attitude, a mistaken zeal. The Grail thus diminishes in thematic importance as it comes down in the tradition, and in this process loses entirely its original mystical tone.

In the light of this general statement it becomes obvious that the three writers with whom I am to deal are not working within the historic literary tradition of the Grail; they have rejected the increasing secularism that has developed within the Grail tradition and in doing so have deliberately returned to a notion of the importance of the Grail in the progress of Arthur's kingdom which is much closer in tone to the Vulgate Cycle than to Tennyson. The reasons for such a reëmphasizing of the older Grail tradition would seem to me to be clear. These writers are all Anglo-Catholics; and two of them, Eliot and Williams, are at times mystical in their approach to religion. Their concept of the essential Faith of the Church of England is thus far removed from that of Tennyson. Furthermore, as I have said in the first chapter of this study, they all have attempted to find in myth some sort of order and certainty to which they may turn in the midst of a disordered age. Thus it is natural that in working with the Arthurian story these three writers should see it (1) in religious terms and (2) as myth. It is natural also that in reshaping the Arthurian materials they should turn their main attention to that version of the story which offers the greatest possibilities for a primarily religious interpretation and for a unification of theme and action.

Two of the three writers, Lewis and Williams, found such a version in Malory's *Morte Darthur* and the third, Eliot, retreated even further into the mystical tradition by using Chrétien's version, which, from Eliot's point of view, could be interpreted as being thematically autonomous and thus open to a mythical rather than a legendary interpretation. Certainly, Malory's whole tale can be regarded as unified; certainly, also, there would seem to be decided hints in Malory that, to use Williams' phrase, the "passage of the Grail destroyed the kingdom." Although Malory's *Morte Darthur* obviously lacks much of the French *Queste*'s mysticism, it may be strongly maintained that Malory discards only the unessential and nonthematic theological material of the French book in order to adapt his source—which, we remember, was essentially an isolated quest—to the unified history of the Arthurian court which he was writing. The only changes Malory makes are thus necessary to his general purpose of unifying the Arthurian story; they do not necessarily result from the fact that Malory was incapable of understanding fully the religious emphasis of his source.

If the Grail is considered to be at the center of the myth as it appears in Malory (and it is clear that Williams, Lewis, and Eliot are working from this interpretation), then the Lancelot-Guinevere theme becomes not a central issue, but a condition that is generally symptomatic of the confusion and failure of secular standards of morality which are brought about by the

35

inability of the Arthurian court to unite religion and civil government. I do not wish to imply that this religious interpretation of Malory is necessarily the correct interpretation or that it can be thought of as necessarily representing Malory's own attitude toward his subject matter. I do wish to insist, however, that this is the interpretation that Williams, Lewis, and Eliot adopt for artistic use. In rejecting the secular emphasis of *The Idylls of the King* and in returning to Malory and Chrétien, these men are attempting, as I have said, to find some sort of controlled and ordered metaphor, basically religious, which they can impose upon their own artistic creations in order to rearrange and unify contemporary experience. Each is attempting to use the Arthurian myth as sacramental metaphor to order his own artistic recreation of experience; to do this, each abstracts from the myth its controlling symbols and uses them to suggest the whole meaning of the myth from which they came. Thus, as we shall see, Williams recreates the myth in terms of the imposition of order (the Emperor, the Grail) upon a rapidly extending chaos (the secular kingdom of Arthur); Lewis abstracts from the myth those symbols (the Pendragon, Merlin, the Fisher King) which he can utilize in presenting a modern equivalent of the battle between Logres and Britain, religion and secularism; Eliot uses the fertility-sterility symbolism of the Grail myth as it appears in Chrétien to control and order a poem dealing with the sterility of a contemporary waste land. None of these writers, it will be seen, uses the Arthurian material as story; each recreates and uses the myth by adapting to his own purposes its major symbols and basic theme.

One further question, however, needs to be discussed: Why do these writers all concentrate upon the Arthurian myth? Although I intend to investigate this question in connection with each of the individual writers concerned, at least three general and immediate reasons are worthy of note here. First, the Arthurian myth is to these writers basically a Christian myth and, as Christian writers, it is natural that they should concentrate on a Christian myth in order to present themes that deal with interpretations of Christian dogma. Second, the Arthurian myth is a part of the native English literary tradition and is therefore extremely useful in developing themes that contrast past and present conditions in British life. Last, the Arthurian myth has as its basis a contrast between order and chaos which becomes, in one set of terms, the failure of secular order to maintain its own existence against the onslaught of the natural and destructive passions. Religion, in the form of the Grail, could have saved Arthur's kingdom, but the Grail was lost and the court crumbled under the weight of lechery, instability, and civil war. It is this last quality of the Arthurian myth which recommends it most highly to modern writers. Certainly, the three writers with whom I am dealing see their basic themes in precisely these terms. Modern Britain between two wars saw the failure of traditional morality in both its private and political life; the British were forced to compromise on all sides. At home, Eliot's clerk and typist seemed to the writers of the period to symbolize most accurately the prevailing moral climate; abroad, England, governed by a policy of appeasement, was forced to abandon her traditional policy of national honor. Traditional morality on all levels seemed to have given way to an easy moral relativism. It is no wonder, then, in the midst of such a moral and political atmosphere, that writers should have sought some order in the midst of disorder, some stability in a world of shifting values. Three of them found their own situations mirrored in the myth of a crumbling civilization, a civilization destroyed by the same sort of secularism which they found everywhere about them in their daily lives. One of them, Charles Williams, set out to recreate this Arthurian myth in exactly these terms; to his reworking of the myth we can at this point turn.

37

3

Charles Williams

CHARLES WILLIAMS' Arthurian poems constitute his own recasting of the Arthurian myth as he derived it from earlier sources, principally Malory. His unfinished prose essay, *The Figure of Arthur,* is, however, a retracing of the myth through all the principal early texts and, though undated, can, I think, be presumed to follow the poetry in Williams' career.[1]

The Figure of Arthur is in many ways a puzzling document. It is apparently a partial first draft, filled with Williams' notes for later additions and corrections. Moreover, there are indications that the completed work would have been a vastly more complex book than the present version would indicate. A "List of Contents" compiled by Williams and introduced by C. S. Lewis from his own collection of Williams' papers allows not only for a history of the development of the Matter of Britain up to and including Malory, but also for a later history of the legend, notably in Spenser and in the eighteenth and nineteenth centuries and possibly, in the two final chapters entitled "The Matter of Britain" and "Galahad," for Williams' prose version of his own reworking of the myth.

Lewis, however, dismisses this List of Contents as irrelevant to an understanding of Williams' intentions on the grounds that it disagrees with the document as Williams left it and with a short "Prefatory Note" to the whole book, also in Lewis' possession. Lewis, I think, is perhaps hasty in dismissing the List of Contents, since the Prefatory Note stands much closer to the List of Contents than to *The Figure of Arthur* as we now have it. The Table of Contents prefacing the existing *Figure of Arthur* takes the following form:

I. The Beginnings
II. The Grail
III. The Coming of the King
IV. The Coming of Love
V. The Coming of the Grail

The List of Contents that Lewis has in his possession is markedly different:

1. The Origin of the Figure
2. The Celtic Tales
3. Geoffrey of Monmouth
4. The Great Inventions
5. The Tudor Revival
6. Malory
7. Spenser
8. The Augustans and Romantics
9. The Victorians
10. The Matter of Britain
11. Galahad

Allowing for the obvious misplacing of chapters five and six, the plan is clear. Now for the Prefatory Note:

This book is a consideration of the tale of King Arthur in English literature. It does not pretend to investigate, or indeed to record, the original sources, the Celtic tales or the French romances, except in so far as some mention of them is necessary to the main theme. That theme is the coming of two myths, the myth of Arthur and the myth of the Grail; of their union; and of the development of that union not only in narrative complexity but in intellectual significance. The book begins with the earliest appearances of both and traces them to the great English presentation in Malory. Malory, however, as we at present have him, never quite fulfilled the hints of profound meaning which are scattered through him. After Malory the political effort of Henry VII to derive his dynasty from Arthur distracted attention from the Grail, and there came the modified Arthur of Spenser. It was not until the nineteenth century that both the king and the Grail began seriously to return, and the great Victorians are shown as labouring to re-express a text their ancestors had defaced. Even they, however, tended (as in general we do to-day) to regard the Lancelot-Guinevere story as more important than that of the Grail; or if not, certainly to regard them as in conflict. In one sense, this must inevitably be so; but in another it is not so at all. The great invention of Galahad is as much of a union and a redemption as of a division and a destruction. It is his double office with which the book is concerned, and the final chapter discusses the developed significance of the whole myth. (*AT* 93–94)

It will be seen that both the List of Contents and the Prefatory Note introduced by Lewis allow for a considerable discussion of the development of the legend after Malory. In both cases, moreover, Williams' general remarks concerning his own reconstructed Arthuriad stand after the historical discussions. In *The Figure of Arthur,* however, Williams' reworking of the myth quite obviously begins toward the end of the final chapter, called "The Coming of the Grail," and before the proposed historical survey had reached either the French chroniclers or Malory. If there is no tremendous hiatus in the text as we have it, and there is no reason to suppose that one of such length would exist, then we must have nearly all of *The Figure of Arthur,* though not all, to judge from the other two documents, of what was to be Williams' complete prose discussion. Thus, it seems to me wise to assume that *The Figure of Arthur* as we have it reprinted here is not a first draft of the final work, but is itself a general plan that Williams wished to expand later along the more orderly and thorough lines indicated in the List of Contents and the Prefatory Note which Lewis brings forward.

I labor this point in order to indicate how much of his prose treatment of the myth Williams left unwritten. Out of a proposed eleven chapters, we have material that would at best cover four of them.[2] Moreover, the little we have (less than a dozen pages) of Williams' reconstruction of the whole myth is so remarkably condensed that it seems almost like a collection of hurried notes for a later expansion. As it stands, however, the purpose of *The Figure of Arthur* is perfectly clear: Williams wishes by means of this essay to ground his own myth in tradition by setting his Arthuriad within the framework of the historical legend. His intention is apparent even in the Prefatory Note where he states his theme to be the "coming of two myths, the myth of Arthur and the myth of the Grail; of their union; and of the development of that union" (*AT* 93). Williams thus establishes immediately that the Grail is to him the thematic core of the Arthurian material and that the historical myth assumes meaning to him only when it focuses on the Grail. The fact that we today tend "to regard the Lancelot-Guinevere story as more important than that of the Grail," Williams takes to be a matter of historical accident. Thus, he sets out in *The Figure of Arthur* to restore what he considers to be the proper emphasis and equilibrium.

The Figure of Arthur begins with a fairly routine though remarkably complete account of "The Beginnings" of the legend. This short first chapter deals only with Gildas, Nennius, *Annales Cambriae*, and those saints' lives that mention Arthur. The second chapter, called simply "The Grail," seeks to find the reasons for the origin of the Grail legend in the historical situation in Europe in the early Middle Ages. Here can be found the germs of ideas that have a great deal to do with Williams' notion of the whole myth. First of all, Williams here, as in other places, maintains for the Grail an exclusively Christian origin:

> Cup or dish or container of whatever kind, the Grail in its origin entered Europe with the Christian and Catholic Faith. It came from and with Christ, and it came with and from no one else. The Eucharist, in Europe, was earlier than any evidence of the fables; that is a matter of history. But then it is a matter of history also that the Eucharist, as it came from and with the whole Christ, was meant for the whole man. (*AT* 23)

Such a view of the origin of the Grail is necessary for an understanding of the place and function of the Grail within Williams' remade myth. The union of Arthur and the Grail, as we shall see, becomes to Williams a gigantic and complex symbol of the union of civilization and Christianity. The attempt to unite the Grail and the Kingdom can almost be called a "type" (to use Williams' term) of the Second Coming. Thus a folklorist or ritual view of the Grail as "cauldron of plenty" or "vessel of magic" (*AT* 13) would lead to a misinterpretation of one of Williams' major symbols and themes.

In this second chapter, Williams lays the foundation of the Grail myth just as he had done with the myth of Arthur in the first chapter. Williams does so by tracing the rise of the Blessed Sacrament to a position of great prominence in the intellectual activity of Europe:

> But as the Nature of our Lord was defined, . . . so the intellectual problems of that Act were more and more discussed. It was stressed now one way and now another; but no stress necessarily denied another. It was a symbol, but it was He. It was the offering of His passion, and communion with His ascended life; also it was communion with His

42

passion and an offering of His ascended life. This was His very death; it was also His very Resurrection; it was, all ways, His Incarnation. (*AT* 14) Williams rehearses the recorded visions connected with the Sacrament, the arguments over Real Presence, the changes in ritual, the final statement of the doctrine of Transubstantiation by the Lateran Council of 1215, and the establishment of the Feast of Corpus Christi by Urban IV in 1264. By means of this historical account, Williams clears the way for the appearance of the Grail by tracing the development of the doctrine that gave it meaning and for which it became both instrument and symbol.

Having made general preparations in his first two chapters for the emergence of the two myths, Williams then in chapters called "The Coming of the King," "The Coming of Love," and "The Coming of the Grail" traces briefly the development of the parts of his intended whole. The first of these chapters deals with the Arthurian chronicle tradition from Geoffrey of Monmouth through Wace and Layamon. The information Williams brings forward is, for the most part, common knowledge, but a few of his interpretations of the Arthurian materials warrant discussion, since within Williams' account of the medieval story lie the seeds of his own remade myth.

First of all, Williams makes the point that the early Middle Ages, roughly defined as pre-thirteenth century, were "founded on metaphysics, but . . . hardly as yet built up into metaphysics" (*AT* 24). There was certainly loyalty to the Church, but as yet that loyalty had not been tested in terms of allegiance to points of doctrine. The Church, for the most part, "except for that one important point of loyalty, left a man to think for himself, and did not much feel it mattered what he thought" (*AT* 25). Thus the twelfth century "was still free to use its imagination in ways which would afterwards be checked or darkened or even elucidated—for example, courtly love, witchcraft, and the Holy Eucharist" (*AT* 25), all of which are of importance in the growth of the Arthurian myth. During this period, according to Williams, discussion of the nature of the Blessed Sacrament was most prevalent in Europe. "This is not to say that it was argued about in every place where men talked. But it was very likely to be spoken—if not argued—about in any place where the intellectuals talked" (*AT* 15). It was in the twelfth century also that Geoffrey of Monmouth set down in great detail the first full version of the Arthur story; Geoffrey "first made Arthur a king. He gave him magnificence and a court. The grey tales suddenly became a diagram of glory" (*AT* 26–27). Williams' point is that the first full blossoming of the Arthurian myth occurred during a period of comparative intellectual freedom, a freedom that made possible the beginnings of two traditions—courtly love and the Grail—which might, had they arisen in later times, have been judged heretical or profane and so perished.

The summary of Geoffrey which follows in *The Figure of Arthur* is routine except perhaps for a brief mention of the Byzantine Empire, which later assumes importance in the poetic cycle. In discussing Arthur's Roman wars, Williams remarks:

> The seat of the imperial power in Byzantium is not mentioned; the king is to be concerned with the west. By Geoffrey's day, of course, the Empire was divided, and yet still theoretically one. But it was as if he had enough historic sense to remember that in his Arthur's own supposedly historic day, it was not so. The king is not allowed to make war on the Emperor himself. (*AT* 30)

In Williams' remade myth, Logres, Arthurian Britain, is the westward limit of the Byzantine Empire, which is a symbol of order, unity, and purpose; its Emperor is "operative Providence." It will be seen from the above quotation that Williams is attempting here in *The*

Figure of Arthur to find for his symbol of the Empire an historical basis, a resting place in fact based on the assumption that although Arthur might conceivably have gone to war with Lucius, he would never have attempted a clash with the Byzantine Emperor. All this is, of course, Williams' assumption; we cannot say what Geoffrey did or did not intend. Yet if Williams' statement is not good historical analysis, it is nevertheless skillful mythmaking.

Williams proceeds to investigate the figure of Merlin as Geoffrey draws him in order to demonstrate as he did with the figure of the Byzantine Emperor how the seeds of his own interpretation of the myth are present in the soil of the early legend. Williams lays chief stress on Merlin's supernatural power, on his knowledge and gift of prophecy, and on his supernatural birth. Thus, it is not at all surprising to find in Williams' poetry that Merlin through this power becomes the agent of reconciliation between Arthur's civilization and the Grail.

In Williams' discussion of Wace and Layamon also we may observe Williams emphasizing those elements of the story which he is later to use in the poetry. Here he concentrates on the invention of the Round Table and especially on Guinevere's treachery, which he insists was an offense not only against Arthur, but also "against chastity and loyalty" (*AT* 43). The virtue of chastity is of great importance to Williams; to him, it is "more than a negation of lust; it is a growing, heightening, and expanding thing. It is a state of spiritual being, and its spiritual expression is not at all inconsistent with marriage" (*AT* 42). Williams attributes great powers to chastity. It is "the means by which all evils are defeated, the flesh is transmuted, and a very high and particular Joy ensured. . . ."[3] In pointing out the place of chastity in theology, Williams says that "the chief name of all [the] balance and interchange and union of the Virtues in flesh was Chastity; for Chastity was precisely the name of its union with

45

the Incarnation. . . . Chastity is the obedience to and the relation with the adorable central body. . . ."[4] Thus in Williams' version of the myth, Guinevere's treachery is against not only the secular code but against religious values as well.

In discussing Layamon, Williams refers briefly to the great western forest, sometimes called Broceliande, which appears occasionally in the Arthurian story. In Williams' poetry, the forest becomes of great importance in the geography of Logres as a symbol of Nature. In *The Figure of Arthur*, Williams hints at the symbolic value that he intends to give to Broceliande by stating that "this western forest was to expand on all sides until presently it seemed as if Camelot and Caerleon and even Carbonek were but temporary clearings within it" (*AT* 40).

With the chapter called "The Coming of Love," Williams takes up the contributions of the French romancers, particularly Chrétien de Troyes and Robert de Boron. After citing the richness of background which Chrétien utilizes, Williams begins a discussion of love as it appears in Chrétien:

> It was 'courtly love.' On the other hand the reader who before looking at Chrétien has heard a good deal of this, its manners, its moralities and immoralities, its literature and its effects, may at first when he does look at Chrétien be a little surprised to find that it is not only real and recognizable but even respectable. The *Lancelot* may, for the moment, be excepted from the generalization. But the *Erec* depends upon a married relationship; the whole question is of the effect of a state of settled love upon a man's proper activities. (*AT* 49)

It will be seen that Williams' construction of courtly love is not the usual one. According to more accepted explanations, courtly love has for one of its prerequisites an adulterous union. C. S. Lewis lists adultery as one of the "characteristics" of the system; ". . . this love, though neither playful nor licentious in its expression, is always what the nineteenth century called 'dishonorable' love. The poet normally addresses another man's wife, and the situation is so carelessly accepted that he seldom concerns himself much with her husband; his real enemy is the rival."[5] Chrétien's *Erec,* which Williams cites as an example of "respectable" courtly love, Lewis calls a work in which the "rules of love and courtesy are outraged at every turn. It is indeed a love story; but it is a story of married love."[6] Indeed the codifier of the system of courtly love, Andreas Capellanus, reports that Marie de Champagne, the patron of the system, ruled in a Court of Love dispute that a true courtly love relation could not exist between husband and wife.

A little later, however, Williams seems to shift ground slightly and clarify his original point.

> The physical beauty of Guinevere appeared to him [Lancelot] a thing literally transcendental. . . . The body of the beloved appears vital with holiness; the physical flesh is glorious with sanctity— not her sanctity, but its own. It is gay and natural to genuflect to it. . . . That [love] sometimes led —and leads—to adultery no more disproves its validity than the fact that it may lead to marriage or renunciation proves it. (*AT* 54–55)

It is clear, I think, that Williams' interpretation of courtly love is closely allied with his conception of the spiritual nature of chastity. These two ideas—the one physical, the other spiritual—combine to form what Williams generally calls Love—or, more exactly, Beatrician love, the semimystical experience celebrated by the *dolce stil nuovo* poets in Italy:

> Eve, Beatrice, or whoever, is certainly her peculiar and (in vision) indefectible self. But she is also the ordinary girl exalted into this extraordinary; she is the norm of all ladies, even if the others do not seem (in the lover's vision) to reach it. The

47

union of flesh and spirit, visible in her (or him),
is credible everywhere; indeed that union . . . is
understood as more profound and more natural
than the dichotomy . . . which has separated
them. She is inclusive of both, and exclusive of
their separateness.[7]

Thus C. S. Lewis says:

The Beatrician experience may be defined as
the recovery (in respect to one human being) of
the vision of reality which would have been common to all men in respect to all things if Man had
never fallen. The lover sees the Lady as the Adam
saw all things before they foolishly chose to experience good as evil, to 'gaze upon the acts in
contention'. (*AT* 116)

It will be seen that courtly love, or at least that phase
of it which enobles the lover and elevates the loved
one, can very well fit into Williams' vision. Yet even
here in *The Figure of Arthur*, Williams prefigures the
aberrations of the Beatrician vision which he develops
in the poetry. The Beatrician experience of Lancelot
fades into mere sensuality:

At the moment when Lancelot bent and pulled the
bars of the window of the queen's room, it was
determined that, for all the courtly conventions in
which it was begun, it was to be a business of
sensuality as well as of adoration. Unless any
greater genius interfered with that development,
the sensual passion would be likely to grow. No
greater genius did. (*AT* 59)

Williams' last chapter, "The Coming of the Grail,"
serves two important functions. It hints at the nature
of the promised unification of the two myths and it
furnishes us with at least the beginning of Williams'
prose reworking of his remade Arthuriad which underlies the two volumes of poetry. Williams lists five
stages in the development of the Grail material up to
Malory.

i) The determination of the Grail as a subject, and the invention of its history.

ii) The relation of this—at first generally; then definitely through Merlin—with the figure of King Arthur.

iii) The invention of the Dolorous Blow.

iv) The development of the love of Lancelot and Guinevere.

v) The invention of Galahad. (*AT* 62–63) Strangely enough, Williams' discussion does not follow this outline. Perhaps a revision would have clarified the order of the discussion, but as the document stands Williams abandons this plan, seemingly in order to prompt a more general discussion, and then midway in this general discussion (he never touches on the last two items in his list) he begins his own unfinished account of the whole myth.

Williams begins his discussion of the development of the Grail with the *Conte del Graal*, or at least of that portion of it dealing with Perceval's adventures in the Grail castle. In discussing the *Conte del Graal*, Williams interjects three comments that have considerable bearing on his own remade myth. First, he suggests that the Fisher King's wound in the thighs is a "wound in the whole virility, spiritual as well as physical" (*AT* 65). Second, Williams points out that the lance and the Grail are "different in kind from what preceded them":

There had been (the scholars tell us) Celtic lances that flamed, but there was no Celtic lance that bled. There had been (they also tell us) vessels and cauldrons which produced physical food; but the Grail in Chrétien did not produce physical food. The whole and exact point of its use was that it provided a substitute for physical food. . . . It served an unknown personage with a Host; if it was like anything, it was like the ciborium of the Eucharist, and contained the super-substantial food. (*AT* 65)

The third comment has to do with Perceval's failure to ask the saving question at the Grail Castle, a failure that Williams ascribes to the "sense of guilt precluding an enquiry into apparent sanctity" (*AT* 66) since it seems to him that the first of the ostensible reasons given by Chrétien—the respect for Gournemant's advice—seems too slight a cause for such a serious failure. Instead, Williams interprets the story to mean that Perceval's failure is caused by his "callous impatience" with his mother. He is thus guilty of a "natural but unhallowed impulse which fails before holiness" (*AT* 66); in short, I think, original sin.

Williams then traces the development of the Grail legend in Chrétien's continuators, whose main contribution, to Williams, is twofold. First, they identify the Grail and lance with the Christian tradition and so allow for the "unifying and heightening" (*AT* 67) of images. Second, they make specific the "great good," left undefined by Chrétien, which Perceval would have brought about had he asked the question at the Grail Castle. This "great good" is defined by the invention of the Waste Land, and the sterility and wounding of the Fisher King, again simply mentioned by Chrétien, is explained by the invention of the Dolorous Blow, which in the remaking of the myth is to become of great importance to Williams as an image of the Fall. Williams, in discussing Chrétien's continuators, clearly shows his attitude toward the whole Matter of Britain. Having said that in one of Chrétien's continuators the entire Table goes from Camelot to the Grail Castle to witness the coronation of Perceval as heir to the guardianship of the Grail, Williams remarks that "it [the journey] is but an episode in one poem, but prophetic of what is happening to the myth. The great Arthurian tradition is already beginning to move towards this other centre" (*AT* 68). Here again, one can see the new myth evolving from the old.

Aside from some remarks concerning the *Perlesvaux*

(Sebastian Evans' *High History*), the rest of Williams' prose survey of the Arthurian materials is denied to us. It can be assumed, however, that he would have next moved on to find his reconciliation in the thirteenth century *La Queste del Saint Graal*, a part of the French Vulgate Prose Cycle, which was Malory's chief source. Here, as later in Malory, the quest for the Holy Grail is one, Williams would say the most important, of the adventures of the Round Table, the adventure in which the Grail is finally achieved by Galahad, the High Prince, who is the son of Lancelot by Elaine, daughter of King Pelles, and thus of the lineage of the guardianship. Lancelot fails in the quest, presumably because of his worldliness, and the kingdom falls, the Grail itself having been transported to Sarras, the land of the Holy Trinity. Exactly how Williams would have interpreted the Prose Cycle *Queste* and Malory we cannot say, except as we can glean an interpretation from the poetry and from a short essay on the figure of Galahad as it appears in Malory. Williams remarks generally of Malory's treatment of the Grail that there is in Malory "a certain suggestiveness which Malory does not seem altogether to have understood";[8] this "suggestiveness" concerns the figure of Galahad. Galahad becomes a synthesis of all the contending forces within the Kingdom; he is the son of Lancelot, he sleeps in the King's bed, he is acceptable even to Guinevere. He is the "living, tragic and joyous Resolution of all their loves."[9]

II

In Williams' reconstructed myth, Arthur is King in Britain, having defeated the "pagan and pirate" forces.[10] For poetic purposes, Williams reduces those many pagan chieftains to a single king, Cradlemas, one-eyed, leering, "a mask o'ergilded" covering "his wrinkled face" (*TTL* 14). The conquest of Britain is quick, decisive:

51

Arthur ran; the people marched; in the snow
  King Cradlemas died in his litter; a screaming
    few
  fled; Merlin came; Camelot grew.
In Logres the king's friend landed, Lancelot of
    Gaul. (*TTL* 15)
"At this time the center of the Roman *imperium* lay in
Byzantium. The Empire was Christian, and not only
Christian but orthodox and Trinitarian. . . . The Pope
was in possession of Rome; about both his figure and
that of the remote Emperor in Byzantium there lay
something of a supernatural light—at best mystical, at
worst magical." (*AT* 79–80) The great schism had not
yet come about; Christendom was as yet whole. This
unity is of primary importance to Williams' scheme.
The Empire is the organic whole upon which all parts
of the myth depend; the Emperor represents "operative
Providence." The Empire as it exists to the east of
Arthur's kingdom (consistently called Logres by Williams) is seen by Williams as organic, whole, an
"anatomical myth." The end leaves of *Taliessin through
Logres* demonstrate this concept graphically. Here the
figure of a woman is superimposed upon a map of
Europe and the Near East. In the drawing, the head of
the woman covers Logres, the breasts France, the hands
Rome, the navel Byzantium, the loins Jerusalem, the
buttocks Caucasia. Finally at the feet lies P'o-lu, the
realm of the headless Emperor, Williams' Hell. The
poem called "The Vision of the Empire" makes clear
the geographical symbolism:
  The organic body sang together;
  dialects of the world sprang in Byzantium;
  back they rang to sing in Byzantium;
  the streets repeat the sound of the Throne.
                                    (*TTL* 6)
Caucasia is the province (in Williams' terminology,
a "theme") of the flesh:

The Empire's sun shone on each round mound,
double fortalices defending dales of fertility.
The bright blades shone in the craft of the dancing
war;
the stripped maids laughed for joy of the province,
bearing in themselves the shape of the province. . . . (*TTL* 7)

Logres is the "head" of the "design," the appointed
place of union:
South from the sea-bone, Thule, the skull-stone,
herbage of lone rock,
the scheme of Logres, the theme of the design of
the Empire,
rose in balance and weight, freight of government
with glory. (*TTL* 7–8)

France gives the milk of learning:
The milk rises in the breasts of Gaul,
trigonometrical milk of doctrine.
Man sucks it; his joints harden,
sucking logic, learning, law,
drawing on the breasts of *intelligo* and *credo*.
(*TTL* 8)

Rome's hands are those of the Pope:
hands of incantation changed to hands of adoration,
the quintuple psalm, the pointing of Lateran:
active and passive in a single mystery,
a single sudden flash of identity,
the heart-breaking manual acts of the Pope.
(*TTL* 9)

In P'o-lu walks the headless Emperor:
Phosphorescent on the stagnant level
a headless figure walks in a crimson cope,
volcanic dust blown under the moon.
A brainless form, as of the Emperor,
walks, indecent hands hidden under the cope.
. . . (*TTL* 11–12)

The rest of the anatomical myth is easily seen. The navel, the organic center, is at Byzantium and the birth-giving loins at Jerusalem.

This symbolic geography, however, does not represent ingenuity for its own sake. The notion of organic order is essential to Williams' myth. The prevailing images connected with the Empire are those of order:

> The Empire lay in the imposed order; around
> the Throne the visionary zone of clear light
> hummed with celestial action; there the forms
> of chamberlains, logothetes, nuncios, went and
> came,
> diagrams of light moving in the light. . . . (SS 3)

And again:

> Carbonek, Camelot, Caucasia,
> were gates and containers, intermediations of light;
> geography breathing geometry, the double-fledged
> Logos. (TTL 1)

Even in the mob at Arthur's coronation, Williams sees order:

> Taliessin in the crowd beheld the compelled
> brutes,
> wildness formalized, images of mathematics,
> star and moon, dolphin and pelican,
> lion and leopard, changing their measure.
> (TTL 20)

Thus Williams perceives order even in the roundness of the flesh. Phoebus' body appears to the young court poets as:

> 'Skeined . . . the creamed-with-crimson sphere
> on a guessed and given line,
> skeined and swirled on the head-to-heel,
> or the radial arms' point-to-point;
> reckoned the rondures of the base
> by the straight absolute spine.' (TTL 28)

To the pagan Palomides, Iseult's rounded arm can be defined only in terms of its hidden straightness:

Blessed (I sang) the Cornish queen;
for till to-day no eyes have seen
how curves of golden life define
the straightness of a perfect line,
till the queen's blessed arm became
a rigid bar of golden flame. . . . (*TTL* 34–35)

Thus it is that the two great outward enemies of the
Empire, P'o-lu and Islam (the denial of the Incarnation) are defined in images of chaos and disorder:

rudiments or relics, disappearing, appearing,
live in the forlorn focus of the intellect,
eyes and ears, the turmoil of the mind of sensation.

Inarticulate always on an inarticulate sea
beyond P'o-lu the headless Emperor moves. . . .
(*TTL* 12)

This Catholic and unified world lies to the east of
Logres. To the west lies the forest of Broceliande. To
Williams, this is the great forest of begettings, of
potentialities, Nature itself. It is a forest, "dangerous to
men" (*SS* 9); there "divine science" and "grand art"
live together in "correspondence." Those few who enter
the forest

come rarely again with brain unravished
by the power of the place—some by grace dumb
and living, like a blest child, in a mild and holy
sympathy of joy; but the rest loquacious with a
    graph
or a gospel, gustily loquacious over three heavens.
(*SS* 9)

Thus, the man who enters Broceliande may become a
saint or a crank; he cannot remain unchanged by his
experience. The ruler of the forest is Nimue, "the
mother of making" (*SS* 13). Greatly changed from
Malory's trickster, Nimue the "mother of all operation"
(*SS* 18) acts as a point of contact between earth, which
Williams conceives platonically as the place of "riven

truths," and heaven, the "climax tranquil" of "unriven truths" (SS 14), which lies in the region of the summer stars. Nimue's children are Merlin and Brisen (the nurse of Helayne, mother of Galahad, who in Malory drugs Lancelot and so brings about the conception of the High Prince) who in Williams' scheme become twins; "they would come then almost like Time and Place to their mission, to prepare in Carbonek and Camelot for the moment of the work" (AT 82):

> Time and space, duration and extension . . .
>   Taliessin
> felt before him an accumulation of power
> tower in the two shapes. . . . (SS 11)

Within Broceliande lies also Carbonek, the resting place of the sacred Grail and lance. Although Carbonek is, strictly speaking, outside of the Empire as Williams conceives it, its presence is as important to Williams' myth as Byzantium. For the union Merlin and Brisen prepare through Arthur and Galahad is the union of Carbonek and Byzantium at Camelot. The union itself becomes a joining and fusion (equivalent to a preparation for the Second Coming) of the religious and civil ideals, of Christianity and the perfect earthly civilization.

> The immediate expectation of the Second Coming had faded, but the vision of it remained as it has always remained in the Church. It might be taken that the King Pelles, the Keeper of the Hallows, was at the proper time, when Merlin had brought Arthur into his royalty and Logres had been cleared and established, to emerge from Carbonek into Logres, . . . the prelude of the Second Coming. Logres was to be blessed thus, and he who said Mass in Sarras would say it in Caerleon and Camelot as he did in Jerusalem. (AT 84)

Yet if the union is prepared within Broceliande, the reasons for the failure of the union lie also within that forest, for there King Pelles lies wounded from the

Dolorous Blow and there roams the Invisible Knight whom Balin the Savage sought. The Dolorous Blow becomes within Williams' myth an image of the Fall of Man:

> The Dolorous Blow consisted in the wounding of the royal Keeper of the Hallows with the Sacred Spear. The Spear was that which had wounded the side of Christ, and it bled continually at the point. It was then aimed at the central heart. But when Balin le Sauvage used it, he used it for his own self-preservation. It is this turning of the most sacred mysteries to the immediate security of the self that is the catastrophic thing. . . . Man wounds himself. It is an image of the Fall. . . . (*AT* 85)

To Williams, the Fall was brought on by Man's being tempted to "gaze . . . on the Acts [of God] in contention" (*TTL* 10). God, as Boethius formulated the doctrine, possesses foreknowledge but is free from any responsibility for the future action that He sees.[11] Thus, to Williams, Evil exists, known to God from the beginning, but known to Him by "simple intelligence," that is, knowledge that is not dependent upon experience. Such knowledge is, of course, denied to Man; to know, Man must experience. Thus, when Satan said to Adam, "Let us gaze, son of man, on the Acts in contention," he was, in fact, ordering the creation of Evil, which had hitherto existed only as an unexplored possibility in the mind of God, a "white pulsing shape" creeping behind the Emperor (*TTL* 10).

> Man desired to know schism in the universe. It was a knowledge reserved to God; man had been warned that he could not bear it—'in the day that thou eatest thereof thou shalt surely die.' A serpentine subtlety overwhelmed that statement with a grander promise—'Ye shall be as gods, knowing good and evil.' Unfortunately to be as gods meant, for the Adam, to die, for to know evil, for them,

was to know it not by pure intelligence but by experience.[12]

The effects of the Fall, symbolized by the Dolorous Blow, manifest themselves in the kingdom in terms of dissension and strife:

> . . . Balin the Savage in ignorance kills his own brother Balan, and Balan him. The natural pieties begin to be lost, and there is incivility in the blood. It is in fact the farther externalization of the Wounded King. But the disorder spreads farther. In the first tales Mordred was the king's nephew; in later versions he became the king's son by incest, but unknown incest. The queen Morgause of Orkney, the wife of King Lot, was Arthur's sister. But he does not know this when she comes to the court, and he tempts her to lie with him. The birth of that incestuous union is Mordred, and the fate of the Round Table comes into the world almost before the Table has been established. . . . (*AT* 86)

In the poetry, the connection is even more graphic:

> 'Balin had Balan's face, and Morgause her brother's.
> Did you not know the blow that darkened each from other's?'
>
> 'Balin and Balan fell by mistaken impious hate.
> Arthur tossed loves with a woman and split his fate.
> Did you not see, by the dolorous blow's might,
> the contingent knowledge of the Emperor floating into sight?' (*TTL* 40)

The seeds of failure are thus present even in the founding of the Table. Merlin, at the coronation of Arthur:

> . . . climbed, through the dome of Stephen,
> over chimneys and churches; from the point of Camelot

he looked through the depth to the dome of
>Sophia;
the kingdom and the power and the glory chimed.
>(*TTL* 19)
Here he sees the heraldry of Logres: the crimson and
black of Morgause, the laughing dolphin of Dinadan,
the sacrificial pelican of Bors, Gawain's thistle, Bedi-
vere's rose, Lancelot's lion, the Queen's chalice, the
King's dragon—"hierarchic, republican, the glory of
Logres, / patterns of the Logos in the depth of the sun"
(*TTL* 20). But here also he sees, at the very beginning
of the fulfillment of the plan of union, the failure of the
attempt:

So, in Lancelot's hand, she [the Queen] came
>through the glow,
into the king's mind, who stood to look on his city:
the king made for the kingdom, or the kingdom
>made for the king?
Thwart drove his current against the current of
>Merlin:
in beleaguered Sophia they sang of the dolorous
>blow.

Doom in shocks sprinkled the burning gloom,
molten metals and kindling colours pouring
into the pyre; at the zenith lion and dragon
rose, clawed, twisted, screamed;
Taliessin beheld a god lie in his tomb. (*TTL* 21)

The question Arthur asks is what leads to his failure:
"is the king to be there for the sake of the Grail or not"
(*AT* 83). Arthur chooses wrongly; he yields to the
temptation to power just as Lancelot does to the
temptation of the Queen. Like the King, Lancelot cannot see the whole plan; in Malory's phrase, he "forgot
the promyse and the perfection" of the Grail quest. The
begetting of Galahad is to him a crime against the code
of chivalric honor by which he lives, not, as it must

seem to Williams, the fruit of the joining of the chosen
representatives of Camelot and Carbonek. In Williams'
terms, Lancelot in sleeping with Helayne

> was betrayed . . . by Merlin and Brisen
>> to truth; he saw not; he was false to Guinevere.
>>> (*TTL* 81)

Therefore, at Mass, Balin, the King, and Lancelot see
only their own images in the Host:

> The household kneeled; the Lord Balin the Savage
>> moved
> restless, through-thrust with a causeless vigil of
>> anger;
> the king in the elevation beheld and loved himself
>> crowned;
> Lancelot's gaze at the Host found only a ghost of
>> the Queen. (*TTL* 47)

Thus, Broceliande contains the seeds of both good
and evil, the success and the failure, Sarras and P'o-lu.
Merlin knows this and so can see, from the beginning,
both the Fall and the Redemption. He tells Taliessin:

> If in the end anything fail of all
> purposed by our mother and the Emperor, if the
>> term
> be held less firm in Camelot than in Carbonek,
> as well my sister and I may guess now
> and prepare the ambiguous rite for either chance
> in the kingdom of Arthur. . . . (*SS* 19)

Thus he "sets the empty chair among all the chairs"
for Galahad who can accomplish the union for himself
if not for the kingdom. Merlin also prepares a remnant
that, if the union fail, may "follow in Logres and
Britain the spiritual roads / that the son of Helayne
shall trace westward through the trees / of Broceliande"
(*SS* 19), a remnant that may bring out of "mere Britain"
a new Logres.

But let us return to the myth itself. Arthur is crowned
amidst great joy to all save Merlin, who sees from his
post atop St. Stephen's dome the seeds of chaos:

Morgause, the unborn Mordred, Lancelot and Guinevere; "in beleaguered Sophia they sang of the dolorous blow."

From this point onward, Williams departs from the usual accounts of chivalry and love and turns his attention to the Grail quest and to those who function as principals in that quest. The King himself becomes, in Williams' phrase, the "passive" center (*AT* 87) of the kingdom. True, Williams modifies the phrase by saying that while he is indeed "no such poor thing," "he does not *seem* to act." Within Williams' poetic cycle, as indeed in almost all of the later accounts of the legend, Arthur is not an active force; in fact, he seems to be at times the least impressive figure in the myth. With Malory, Lancelot assumes the place of the Great Knight, but even before Malory, others—Gawain, Cador—had tended to usurp the King's prominence. Williams, however, does add one touch to the figure of Arthur— personal vanity—which is new to the myth. Arthur's rejection of the true answer to the question "the king made for the kingdom, or the kingdom made for the king?" shows this vanity clearly as does the passage, already quoted, wherein Arthur sees his own glory reflected in the Host. Then too, it is clear that Arthur is in many ways guilty of one of Williams' major sins, spiritual incest, called Gomorrah in the novels, in which a man withdraws entirely into himself, neglecting both his civil and religious duties, possessed by cupidity, the love of self, as opposed to charity, the love of others. Arthur, in sleeping with his own image, has committed spiritual incest, has entered Gomorrah. The product of the union is Mordred, the destroyer.

Lancelot becomes, then, the "active centre" of the kingdom; "he affirms friendship, courtesy, justice, and nobility" (*AT* 87). Yet, as in Malory, he too is a sinful man and, as with Arthur, his sin helps to bring on the dissolution of the kingdom. Williams implies that like Arthur, Lancelot forgets his proper function in the state in order to appropriate something that is not rightly his, Queen Guinevere.

Guinevere assumes in Williams' work her traditional role of unfaithful queen. Her failure may, in past legend, have been forced upon her by her position at the court:

> Guinevere has always been a slight difficulty, for in the situation of the tale, she has nothing to do but to be in love with Lancelot. He can ride out, and have adventures, and return, but she can only sit and work at embroideries and love. (*AT* 88)

Yet again, Williams adds here a new strain to the traditional character: Guinevere is condemned for what we might best call levity; the queen cannot realize or maintain the seriousness of her position as a queen and a model of womankind. In a remarkable poem, "Taliessin in the Rose-Garden," the poet, wandering in a garden, prays that:

> . . . the queen's majesty, the feminine headship of Logres,
> deign to exhibit the glory to the women of Logres;
> each to one vision, but the queen for all.
> (*SS* 27–28)

Yet, at the same time, he sees reflected in the blood-red ring that Guinevere wears the red, flowing blood of King Pelles' wound, and, by extension, the blood of Christ on Calvary. Then, through an extension to menstrual blood, he identifies Guinevere with Eve and sees in Guinevere another image of the Fall. Yet it is sure that Guinevere could have overcome this natural sin; certainly, in Williams' poem, Dindrane does. The difference between the women, however, is that Dindrane recognizes her proper function in that she is able, by the laws of Exchange, to give her blood to a dying girl, so sanctifying it, and by that act, dying herself. Guinevere cannot do this. Seeing Taliessin within the garden, she can only say "with the little scorn that becomes a queen of Logres: / 'Has my lord dallied with poetry

62

among the roses?'" (*SS* 28) To Williams, Guinevere herself is forever dallying.

Palomides, the pagan knight, receives unusually full treatment in the cycle. As we shall see, he is to become the model of one sort of Beatrician lover. The difficulty of his conversion is also stressed by Williams since, in his conversion, he represents a common attitude toward Christianity and the Grail. Having turned away from Iseult in an agony of disappointment, he pursues the Blatant Beast, at once the most impossible and most sterile of all the quests. He cannot, of course, win the worldly recognition that he seeks in this quest, and so must search for the approval of the court in yet another fashion—by participation in the great Tournament of Lonazep. Yet as Williams says, "It is there that Palomides does his greatest deeds—'it is his day' said Sir Dinadan—but also his worst; for he overthrows Lancelot by falsehood" (*AT* 90). He retires disappointed to a rocky cave where he is eaten by gnats and mosquitoes. At last, reluctant and humiliated, he rides "to Dinadan" (*TTL* 68). Thus, he finally accepts the system that Dinadan represents not through joy and hardly through conviction, but because it is inevitable that he accept his place, even though he must suffer in doing so.

Palomides stands in violent opposition to Dinadan, the great laugher and japer of Malory. Dinadan very nearly becomes the hero of Williams' myth. Next to Galahad, Talliessin, and Merlin, he is certainly the wisest of the company; he is close to the "laughter at the heart of things." He laughs and japes constantly because he accepts with humility and without question what he sees to be the "excellent absurdity" of the universe. He knows that, in the complex hierarchy of the universe, no single person is indispensable, that all men are expendable. Thus he tells Taliessin:

> To neighbor
> whom and as the Omnipotence wills is a fetch

of grace; the lowest wretch is called greatest
—and may be—on the feast of fools. The God-
    bearer
is the prime and sublime image of entire super-
    fluity.
If an image lacks, since God backs all,
be the image, a needless image of peace
to those in peace; to you an image of modesty.

(SS 41)

Taliessin, through whose eyes we see most of the action, is presumably given prominence in the myth to
fulfill this particular function. Merlin, of course, was
needed for a more important role. Taliessin thus becomes Williams' model poet and through Taliessin it
is possible, as we shall see, to trace many of Williams'
ideas of poetry and myth.

Taliessin's great love is Dindrane (sometimes, through
an oversight, called Blanchefleur [AT 137–138]) the
sister of Perceval. In Williams' account, as in Malory's,
she is most famous for the generous and fatal gift of
her blood to a wounded lady. Yet in the poetry, she
assumes thematic importance; Williams identifies Dindrane with all the women associated with Perceval in
the early history of the Grail quest and thus enlarges
her into a "figure of sanctity, feminine and self-giving"
(AT 70). She becomes, in fact, all that Guinevere should
have been and was not. Thus, she alone of all the women
is privileged to be carried for burial to Sarras, the Land
of the Trinity.

Bors also assumes a new role in Williams' reconstruction of the legend. Bors, in Malory, is the one knight
who is able to experience spiritual development in the
quest of the Holy Grail, the minor knight who, lacking
both Lancelot's greatness and Lancelot's sin, is able to
achieve the Grail by following the path from temporal
values to spiritual values, the path Lancelot is unable
to follow. In Williams, this general point is reinforced
through a well-developed picture of Bors as a citizen of

64

Logres. The quest of the Grail, says Williams, is "the tale of Galahad; it is the tale of the mystical way; but it is also the tale of the universal way. . . . Bors is in the chapel at Sarras as well as Galahad and Perceval. This is what relates the Achievement to every man. The tale must end, and that part of it when the holy thing returns again to earth—when Galahad is effectually in Bors as Bors is implicitly in Galahad—cannot be told until the clause of the Lord's prayer is fulfilled and the kingdom of heaven is come upon earth . . ." (*AT* 84). Thus it is that at the entry of the chosen knights into Carbonek, Bors, as representative of chastened mankind, forgives Galahad for his sanctity, which has driven Lancelot mad, and goes first to meet the angelic household:

> The Infant said: 'Go, cousin.' Bors
> stepped from the arch; the angelic household met him.
> The High Prince stepped in his footprints; into the sun
> Galahad followed Bors; Carbonek was entered.
> (*TTL* 83)

Williams pushes to its logical conclusion a trend already apparent in Malory; he makes Galahad almost completely divine. Williams had listed "the invention of Galahad" as one of the topics to be discussed in the last chapter of *The Figure of Arthur;* however, no connected discussion of Galahad's position in the tradition has come down to us. But it is possible to find hints of what Williams conceived Galahad to be. At one point, we find a reference to his "mystical chastity and . . . single wholeness" (*AT* 72). Williams states that "the figure of the High Prince is for something much more than morals" (*AT* 74). Again, Galahad is identified with the "mystical way" (*AT* 84). In the poetry, he is called "the Merciful Child," "subdued Glory," "the Infant," "the Child," "the alchemical Infant," and at the last Mass, conducted by Lancelot:

65

> Over the altar, flame of anatomized fire,
> the High Prince stood, gyre in burning gyre;
> day level before him, night massed behind;
> the Table ascended; the glories intertwined.
>
> (*TTL* 91)

It is thus strongly hinted that Galahad is perhaps the type of the Second Coming, the New Man in whom "is realized the union which ought to have been realized in Logres as a whole" (*AT* 168). Taliessin tells Gareth:

> 'My lords and fathers the Druids between the hazels
> touched poems in chords; they made tell
> of everywhere a double dance of a stone and a shell
>
> . . .
>
> To-day
> the stone was fitted to the shell,' the king's poet said;
> 'when my lord Sir Lancelot's son sat in the perilous sell. . . .' (*TTL* 70–71)

Thus, Galahad is born, significantly, of the sanctified Helayne and the heroic, though sinful Lancelot under the direction of Time (Merlin) and Space (Brisen). But once Galahad has accomplished the Grail, he has, as Williams says, "necessity of being in himself" (*AT* 178) and so becomes something more than man. After the quest has ended, Galahad must flee Logres, which is now marked for destruction. He cannot be identified with the failure of the kingdom; having personally achieved the Grail, he must depart with it from the stricken Logres.

To return again to the myth itself—having established his geography and defined his characters, Williams moves to reinforce his conception both of the qualities inherent in the union of Camelot and Carbonek and the reasons for the failure of that union. We see nothing of the quest itself, only incidents in the careers of the essential characters—Taliessin and Guinevere in a garden, Taliessin teaching the young poets and slave girls, Dindrane's arrival at court, Mordred meditating on his own ambition. But in every case, the main themes of the cycle are reinforced and examined from varying points of view. To those themes let us now turn, in order to examine the meaning and purpose of Williams' Arthurian cycle.

III

Perhaps the greatest single image that Williams develops in remaking the Arthurian legend is that of organic unity and order. There would seem to be little doubt, moreover, that this is Williams' contribution; order and fact are so much a part of Williams' whole theology that he could hardly have helped seeing the Arthurian world as anything other than an ordered kingdom. The Arthurian world is, as we have noted before, marked by order at every phase of its existence. Yet this concept of order is not exploited in the cycle for its own sake; its presence in Williams nearly always denotes the sacred, the holy. It is therefore fitting that the Empire ruled by Williams' Emperor, "operative Providence," should be based on and reflect Williams' strongly-held notion that "God always geometrizes" and that religion can be best expressed in images of mathematical exactitude. Thus, sin is "the preference of an immediately satisfying experience of things to the believed pattern of the universe; one may even say, the pattern of the glory."[13] Again, he remarks that the word "day" in Genesis becomes a "refrain of mathematical incantation."[14] He states at one point that "the kingdom of heaven will not be defined by inexact terms"[15] and in discussing the Old Testament prophets remarks that these men were "sent out from the visible mathematics of the glory to proclaim the moral mathematics of the glory."[16]

The logic of the Empire thus reflects the order of the universe; Arthurian Logres becomes a microcosm of

the ideal cosmic civilization in which even the devia-
tions from precision, as, for example, the curve of Iseult's
arm, serve to redefine the straightness of the pattern
that permits the curve. Order, in Williams' terms, is
always the mode of God's existence and its manifestations in the world are His handiwork. Thus it is that
when Logres and the Empire begin to crumble, images
of disorder and chaos replace those of geometrical precision. In the description of Morgause of Orkney,
Lamorak says:

> Her hand discharged catastrophe; I was thrown
> before it; I saw the source of all stone,
> the rigid tornado, the schism and first strife
> of primeval rock with itself, Morgause Lot's wife.
> (*TTL* 38)

Bors, in a vision of the fall of the Empire, says:

> . . . I came through the night, and saw the dragon-
> lets' eyes
> leer and peer, and the house-roofs under their
> weight
> creak and break; shadows of great forms
> halloed them on, and followed over falling towns.
> (*TTL* 43)

Mordred sees that:

> London is become a forest; voices and arms
> throw a dementia of hands, tossed caps,
> towzled shouts, bare grinning leaves,
> a whole wood of moral wantons, whose spines
> are tree-stretched up towards me, their hope.
> (*SS* 48)

The Pope, at the end, sees no peace in the Empire:

> A tale that emerged from Logres surged in Europe
> and swelled in the Pope's ears; it held nothing
> of fulfillment of prophecy and the sea-coming of
> the Grail
> but only of bleak wars between Arthur and Lance-
> lot,

68

Gawaine set to seek his heart's vengeance,
the king's son gone whoring with fantasy,
and mobs roaring through Camelot. . . . (SS 51)

Logres thus exists as a temporary ordering of chaos by the Emperor. But this order depends upon mankind for its preservation, and when order disappears the pattern of civilization is broken and chaos returns. Mankind preserves order in his own house by honoring and practicing what is one of God's great natural laws—the law of Substitution or Exchange. C. S. Lewis explains Williams' law of Exchange in this way:

(1) The Atonement was a Substitution, just as Anselm said. But that Substitution, far from being a mere legal fiction irrelevant to the normal workings of the universe, was simply the supreme instance of a universal law. . . . All salvation, everywhere and at all times, in great things or in little, is vicarious. The courtesy of the Emperor has absolutely decreed that no man can paddle his own canoe and every man can paddle his fellow's, so that the shy offering and modest acceptance of indispensable aid shall be the very form of the celestial etiquette. (2) We can and should 'bear one another's burdens' in a sense much more nearly literal than is usually dreamed of. Any two souls can ('under the Omnipotence') make an agreement to do so: the one can offer to take another's shame or anxiety or grief and the burden will actually be transferred. (AT 123)

This doctrine—called indiscriminately Largesse, Exchange, Substitution—represents the working out in daily life of the central doctrines of Christianity, the Incarnation and Atonement, which themselves are manifestations of what Williams called the "co-inherence" of all things, the fact that no single item or action in the universe can be isolated from the web of divine interconnection and interdependence of which it is a part.

Williams takes his principal evidence for the operative effectiveness of the doctrine from Scripture. He says in discussing Cain and Abel:

> Usually the way must be made ready for heaven, and then it will come by some other; the sacrifice must be made ready, and the fire will strike on another altar. So much Cain saw and could not guess that the very purpose of his offering was to make his brother's acceptable.[17]

In discussing the Crucifixion, he says:

> The taunt flung at that Christ, at the moment of his most spectacular impotency, was: 'He saved others; himself he cannot save.' It was a definition as precise as any in the works of the medieval schoolmen. . . . It was an exact definition of the kingdom of heaven in operation, and of the great discovery of substitution. . . .[18]

Thus, life on earth can be made, through Exchange, to resemble life in heaven; "all life is to be vicarious—at least, all life in the kingdom is to be vicarious."[19] To Williams, Substitution is thus a social reflection of the general theological virtue called *caritas* by St. Paul, the love of others not for themselves but for the divine qualities they exhibit, a doctrine that itself stems from the unified point of view imposed by the co-inherence. Its manifestations thus become the social virtues of humility and courtesy.

On one level, *caritas* marks a relationship between God and man, but it can be seen operating, in Williams' view, in the daily actions of men and women. This, then, is the secret of the "excellent absurdity" of the universe which Dinadan sees whereby every man becomes superfluous since every man, in reality, works for another; "my friend's shelter for me, mine for him" (*TTL* 45). It is impossible, moreover, to separate the doctrine of *caritas* from its practice; they are indistinguishable. "The descent of the City [which is a social concept], in its web of exchanged glory, is the definition of the necessary *caritas*, the 'for my sake' of the gospels."[20]

Thus, the interconnection and interdependence of men are not mere catchwords in Williams; they are spiritual facts.

This concept becomes the working system of Logres in Williams' myth. Taliessin, we learn, must do "many a turn of exchange in the need / of himself or others or the Empire" before he can think "in Merlin's style" or "his verse grow mature with pure fact" (SS 15). Upon seeing the magical arts of Merlin and Brisen, "Taliessin / began then to share in the doctrine of largesse / that should mark in Camelot the lovers of the king's poet" (SS 16). Merlin informs the poet that they shall work till "Sarras is free to Carbonek, Carbonek to Camelot; / in all categories holds the largesse of exchange, / and the sea of Broceliande enfolds the Empire" (SS 17). This doctrine of Largesse becomes the rule of the king's poet's company, the household of Taliessin, which will later become the remnant of Logres when Logres sinks into "mere Britain." Its cult

> . . . was the Trinity and the Flesh-taking,
> and its rule as the making of man in the doctrine of
>   largesse,
> and its vow as the telling, the singular and mutual
>   confession
> of the indwelling, of the mansion and session of
>   each in each. (SS 36–37)

The doctrine of Exchange can be seen operating at three levels. First:

> . . . at the first station,
> were those who lived by a frankness of honorable
>   exchange,
> labour in the kingdom, devotion in the Church, the
>   need
> each had of other. . . . (SS 37)

At a second level:

> The Company's second mode bore farther
> the labour and fruition; it exchanged the proper
>   self
> and wherever need was drew breath daily

in another's place, according to the grace of the
Spirit
'dying each other's life, living each other's death.'
(SS 38)
Finally:
Few—and that hardly—entered on the third
station, where the full salvation of all souls
is seen, and their co-inhering, as when the Trinity
first made man in Their image, and now restored
by the one adored substitution; there men
were known, each alone and none alone,
bearing and borne, as the Flesh-taking sufficed
the God-bearer to make her a sharer in Itself.
(SS 39)
Thus, in one poem, we see a multitude of Christian
lovers of poetry rushing to support the pagan Virgil at
the hour of his death. In exchange, his pagan poetry has
helped them to become better Christians:
In that hour they came; more and faster, they sped
to their dead master; they sought him to save
from the spectral grave and the endless falling,
who had heard, for their own instruction, the sound
of his calling. (TTL 32)
Through Exchange, the company develops into a
"labyrinth of vicariousness." At the coming of Galahad,
Taliessin standing outside the castle, sees
through the unshuttered openings of stairs and
rooms
the red flares of processional torches and candles
winding to the king's bed; where instead
of Arthur Galahad that night should lie,
Helayne's son instead of the king's, Lancelot's
instead of Guinevere's, all taken at their word,
their professions, their oaths; the third heaven
heard
their declarations of love, and measured them the
medium of exchange. (TTL 69)
But the doctrine and its application to the myth are

perhaps best seen in a poem entitled "Bors to Elayne: on the King's Coins." Bors, the householder and farmer, returns from "organization" in London to find Elayne busy with the baking of bread. The sight reminds him of the kindly exchange of effort whereby they live:

> I came in; I saw you stand,
> in your hand the bread of love, in your head light-
> ness of law.
> The uprightness of the multitude stood in your
> figure;
> my fieldsmen ate and your women served,
> while you watched them from the high seat.
> (TTL 42)

Elayne's hands become to Bors the means of Exchange:

> Now when the thumbs are muscled with the power
> of goodwill
> corn comes to the mill and the flour to the house,
> bread of love for your women and my men;
> at the turn of the day, and none only to earn;
> in the day of the turn, and none only to pay;
> for the hall is raised to the power of exchange of all
> by the small spread organisms of your hands. . . .
> (TTL 42–43)

London, however, has forgotten this law. Instead of "lightness of law," now Arthur insists on "ration and rule, and the fault in ration and rule, / law and the flaw in law" (*TTL* 43). Arthur adopts the "ration and rule" that are a part of organic order, but fails in neglecting the spirit that should direct the law, whereas Elayne holds the law lightly, without effort, and directs her main attention to the fulfilling of what the law directs, the "organic salvation of our good."

Bors reports that the King has authorized a coinage to facilitate commerce. Kay, traditionally "wise in economics," approves, saying that the new money will control the kingdom better than "the swords of lords or the orisons of nuns." Money, to Kay, is "the medium of exchange." What Bors realizes is that it is an artificial

medium of exchange, a "fallacy of rational virtue."
Thus, he prays that the "new law" may be redeemed.
Taliessin agrees, knowing that the symbols may become
autonomous, that they may become important not as
media for exchange but for themselves and so become
"deadly." The Archbishop quotes the true doctrine:

> '. . . this abides—
> that the everlasting house the soul discovers
> is always another's; we must lose our own ends;
> we must always live in the habitation of our lovers,
> my friend's shelter for me, mine for him.'
>
> (*TTL* 44–45)

What Williams is driving at in this poem and in the
others that deal with Exchange is this: the largesse, the
free giving and taking of one another's efforts and
bounty, must be the law of the kingdom. Once an individual man, through the autonomous wealth of coins,
becomes independent of the group, the co-inherence of
all things is destroyed and the collapse imminent. We
see the effects of Arthur's coinage in "The Meditation of
Mordred":

> The nit-witted wittols or worldly wisdom tear
> their throats at the abolition of the Byzantine trib-
> ute,
> now the coined dragons stay in their pockets at
> home.
> Kin to kin presently, children; I too am a dragon.
>
> (*SS* 48)

Taliessin, of course, was correct; in the end, the symbols became independent; they go no more to Byzantium in exchange. Instead, they find their way into
Mordred's treasury. The doctrine of Exchange has been
abandoned.

Dindrane, the sister of Perceval, is another creature
of Exchange in the poem; she gives her own life blood
to save the sick lady. Thus, she "died another's death,
another lived her life." In the last poem of the cycle,

moreover, all the substitutions are rehearsed and reconciled. Helayne and Guinevere:

> In Blanchefleur's cell at Almesbury the queen Guinevere
> felt the past exposed; and the detail, sharp and dear,
> draw at the pang in the breast till, rich and reconciled,
> the mystical milk rose in the mother of Logres' child. (*TTL* 89)

Arthur and Pelles:

> Out of the queen's substitution the wounded and dead king
> entered into salvation to serve the holy Thing;
> singly seen in the Mass, owning the double Crown,
> going to the altar Pelles, and Arthur moving down.
> (*TTL* 89)

The company of Taliessin:

> . . . my household stood
> around me, bearers of the banners, bounteous in blood;
> each at the earthen footpace ordained to be blessed and to bless,
> each than I and than all lordlier and less. (*TTL* 90)

Christ and Galahad:

> Over the altar, flame of anatomized fire
> the High Prince stood, gyre in burning gyre. . . .
> (*TTL* 91)

Even the evil of P'o-lu can be "retrieved" in the midst of the Emperor's geometry:

> We exposed, We exalted the Unity; prismed shone
> webs, paths, points; as it was done
> the antipodean zones were retrieved round a white rushing deck,
> and the Acts of the Emperor took zenith from Caucasia to Carbonek. (*TTL* 90)

Thus, what should have been accomplished in the ordinary life of Logres can be effected only after the failure of the kingdom and within the operation of the Mass. All is reconciled and exchanged in the final moment, but the Grail has departed, the "parallels," symbols of order, "desecrated" (*TTL* 54).

This doctrine of Exchange threads its way through the cycle. It is clear that Williams in this concept is giving a local habitation and a name to the generalized Christian virtue of charity, which has as its basis the love of God in man. The corresponding sin is, of course, cupidity, Williams' "self-sufficiency," which involves the love of an object, in Williams nearly always the self, for its own sake. Thus, "Bors to Elayne: on the King's Coins" deals with the great danger of collecting and loving the coins, not as media of exchange, but as objects of desire in themselves. Human love in the cycle demonstrates this aspect of the doctrine of Exchange quite clearly.

There are six sets of lovers in the cycle—Taliessin and Dindrane, Bors and Elayne, Palomides and Iseult, Lancelot and Guinevere, Lamorak and Morgause, and Arthur and Morgause—each of them demonstrating a different aspect of Williams' basic concept of Beatrician love. As we have said, the basis of the system lies in the Platonic concept of the recognition and concentration of the lover on both the divine and physical aspects of the beloved. "The lover sees the Lady as Adam saw all things . . ." (*AT* 116). The lover, then, must examine the "pattern of the glory" (*AT* 117) in the beloved and so acknowledge charity rather than cupidity as the basis of his love.

> Beatrice . . . is no longer to be loved for the gratification of the lover, in however pure or passionate a sense. She is no longer to be loved for herself alone. . . . Beatrice is to be loved 'for my sake.'[21]

In the poem, the pure Beatrician state exists in the love of Taliessin and Dindrane. At their first meeting, Taliessin sees and adores Dindrane as the physical image of the Empire's order:

'Blessed is the eyed axis of both horizons,
and the wheel that taxes the hips and generates the
    sphere,
and illumination that waxes in the full revolution.'

Proportion of circle to diameter, and the near
    asymptote
Blanchefleur's smile. . . . (*TTL* 53)

Nor does he ever depart from this conception of her. It is Taliessin's usual habit of mind. In "Taliessin in the School of the Poets," the poet-teacher teaches his students to see the body of the carved Phoebus in terms of its order and symmetry:

The darkened glamour of the golden-work
    took colour from each line;
dimly the gazing postulants saw
patterns of multilinear red
sprinkled and spreading everywhere,
    and spaced to one design. (*TTL* 29)

Again in "The Star of Percivale," we see Taliessin teaching a serving girl the doctrine of largesse. The girl, enraptured by the poet's music, rushes to him "in adoration." He first teaches her to love him not for himself, and then directs her attention to the "pattern of the glory":

The king's poet leaned, catching the outspread
    hands:
More than the voice is the vision, the kingdom than
    the king:
the cords of their arms were bands of glory; the
    harp
sang her to her feet; sharply, sweetly, she rose.
                                    (*TTL* 46)

With Bors and Elayne, we see the Beatrician experience translated from the highly mystical level of Taliessin and Dindrane into ordinary domestic experience.

Again we see the joining of flesh and spirit in the person of the beloved. In the poem called "Bors to Elayne: The Fish of Broceliande," Bors has just returned from duty on the southern coast. There, he "plucked a fish from a stream that flowed to the sea" (*TTL* 24). The fish is used in the poem as a representative of Broceliande itself, the magic, dangerous wood, and thus becomes a symbol of one aspect of Bors's love for Elayne. He gives the fish to Elayne, only to see it become absorbed into her body just as the magic, the spirit, the Broceliande of his love for her becomes indistinguishably entangled with the image of her body:

> . . . shall I drop the fish into your hand?
> into your hand's pool? a bright-scaled, red-tailed
> fish
> to dart and drive up the channel of your arm?
> (*TTL* 24)

Only a "twy-nature," we find, can control the bright fish, call it forth at will. This concept of the "twy-nature," the double nature of things, is another aspect of the co-inherence. In the cycle as a whole, this joining motif acts as a device for the unification of opposing complementary images. It can be seen in the constantly repeated image of the great theme of the poem—the unification of Camelot and Carbonek—and in other lesser images, for example, the joining of the stone and the shell in the person of Galahad. Generally speaking, this act of joining and reconciliation is necessary for the completion of the whole image, as the stone must be fitted to the shell to complete the whole man, Galahad. Within the "excellent absurdity" of the universe, every act is connected with another act that completes it. Here, Bors and Elayne must join to bring the bright fish, love, "from the stirred stream." Yet, even so, the fish is still ambiguous, suggesting as it does the "smooth plane / of the happy flesh" and the martyr's tomb "where the Catacomb's stone / holds its diagram over the happy dead." Thus, as Lewis says, love, to Williams, leads both to "pleasure and to sacrifice" (*AT* 115).

Descending from Bors and Elayne, the perfect earthly lovers, we come to Palomides and Iseult. The pagan knight's first glimpse of the Irish princess shows perfectly Williams' concept of the twy-natured identity of spirit and flesh, straight line and curve:

> Blessed for ever be the hour
> when first the intellectual power
> saw triple angles, triple sides,
> and that proceed which naught divides
> through their great centre, by the stress
> of the queen's arm's blissful nakedness,
> to unions metaphysical. . . . (*TTL* 35)

Yet when Palomides sees that Iseult is Tristram's, he loses the vision:

> Down the arm of the queen Iseult
> quivered and darkened an angry bolt;
> and, as it passed, away and through
> and above her hand the sign withdrew.
> Fiery, small, and far aloof,
> a tangled star in the cedar roof,
> it hung; division stretched between
> the queen's identity and the queen. (*TTL* 36)

He separates the "queen's identity and the queen"; he no longer sees her as Bors saw Elayne, since now he sees her body and soul separately. Thus, he joins the most frustrating of all quests:

> I heard the squeak of the questing beast,
> where it scratched itself in the blank between
> the queen's substance and the queen. (*TTL* 37)

Here we have another symbol of the fall of the Empire. The love chain is broken; like Arthur, who can see the kingdom only in terms of its king, Palomides can see Iseult only in terms of his own desire, his own cupidity. The bond of Exchange must hold on every level within Logres, else it cannot hold at all.

79

Even more serious for the kingdom is the fatal love of Lancelot and Guinevere. These two also are guilty of Palomides' sin, cupidity. They also separate spirit from body. Yet they do what Palomides would not, or at least did not do. They continue to love, in spite of honor and law. Palomides, after his disappointment, goes through a long period of frustration and torment, but the frustration and the torment lead eventually to his conversion and acceptance of the law of Exchange. Lancelot and Guinevere perpetuate their mis-vision by continuing to half-love each other. Thus, another rent is made in the wholeness of the Empire.

The love of Lamorak and Morgause differs in origin. There is no hint of a Beatrician vision here, only chaos:

Ship and sculpture shuddered; the crags' scream
mingled with the seamews'; Logres' convulsed
  theme
wailed in the whirlwind; we fled before the storms,
and behind us loosed in the air flew giant inhuman
  forms.

When from the sea I came again to my stall
King Arthur between two queens sat in a grim hall,
Guinevere on his right, Morgause on his left;
I saw in her long eyes the humanized shapes of the
  cleft. (*TTL* 39)

Why does Lamorak love her? There is no answer in the poem, only the hint that one may become fascinated with evil, as so many characters in Williams' novels do, and so fall in love with it for its own sake. Lamorak is:

. . . the queen's servant; while I live
down my eyes the cliff, the carving, the winged
  things drive,
since the rock, in those fleet lids of rock's hue,
the sculpture, the living sculpture, rose and flew.
                                            (*TTL* 41)

However, the greatest perversion of love in the poem is that of Arthur. Lamorak's love is evil certainly, but it involves another person and so implies some sort of need for others. Arthur's love is for himself and is symbolized in the poem by his incestuous intercourse with Morgause of Orkney:

> Through the rectangular door the crowned shape
> went its way;
> it lifted light feet: an eyeless woman lay
> flat on the rock; her arm was stretched to embrace
> his own stretched arm; she had his own face.
> <div align="right">(<i>TTL</i> 40)</div>

Through their union:

> The child lies unborn in the queen's womb;
> unformed in his brain is the web of all our doom,
> as unformed in the minds of all the great lords
> lies the image of the split Table and of surreptitious
> swords. (<i>TTL</i> 41)

This is Gomorrah in Logres, an image of the Fall and the destruction.

One more theme in the cycle needs to be discussed, though in less detail than the others. This theme involves "the two chief ways of approach to God defined in Christian thought"[22]—the Way of Affirmations and the Way of Rejections. Lewis describes the two approaches in this way:

> Two spiritual maxims were constantly present to the mind of Charles Williams; "This also is Thou" and "Neither is this Thou." Holding the first we see that every created thing is, in its degree, an image of God, and the ordinate and faithful appreciation of that thing a clue which, truly followed, will lead back to Him. Holding the second we see that every created thing, the highest devotion to moral duty, the purest conjugal love, the saint and the seraph, is no more than an image, that every one of them, followed for its own sake and isolated from its source, becomes an idol whose service is damnation. The first maxim is the formula of the Romantic Way, the 'affirmation of images';

the second is that of the Ascetic Way, the 'rejection of images.' Every soul must in some sense follow both. (*AT* 151)

Williams himself says in discussing the history of the Church:

The one Way [to worship] was to affirm all things orderly until the universe throbbed with vitality; the other to reject all things until there was nothing anywhere but He. The Way of Affirmation was to develop great art and romantic love and marriage and philosophy and social justice; the Way of Rejection was to break out continually in the profound mystical documents of the soul. . . .[23]

Certainly, however, the Way of Affirmations is more constantly present in the poem than the Way of Rejections. We are constantly informed of the beauties of the flesh, the "glory of substantial being." Thus Greek philosophy with its sterile logic is defeated by the "physiological glory" of the young Church:

The crooked smiles of the Greeks
fled from their faces while thorned-in-the-flesh the
    Apostle
against their defensive inflections of verb and
    voice,
their accents of presaged frustration, their sterile
    protections,
named in its twyfold Nature the golden Ambiguity.
                                                    (*SS* 1)

And again:

Professing only a moral union, they fled
from the new-spread bounty; they found a quarrel
    with the Empire
and the sustenance of Empire, with the ground of
    faith and earth,
the golden and rose-creamed flesh of the grand
    Ambiguity. (*SS* 2)

Throughout the poem, images of Caucasia, the "rounded

82

bottom of the Emperor's glory" are kept before the reader:

> the flesh and blood, the golden cream and the rose
> tinctures; these dwelled in Byzantium; they were held
> in men and women, or even (as named qualities)
> in the golden day and the rose-gardens of Caucasia. (SS 3)

Taliessin, teaching the Caucasian slave girls and directing their love to God, is the greatest representative of the Way of Affirmations. On the other hand, Dindrane on her way to the nunnery is possibly the greatest representative of the Way of Rejections. Both are necessary to Logres and to the Empire. What this dichotomy points to is another aspect of the twy-nature of the Empire and the co-inherence of the universe. As with the lovers, joining and exchanging loves and bounties in the way of Exchange, as with Galahad in the fitting of stone and shell, as with the joining of Camelot and Carbonek, so here in these two aspects of life, Williams makes clear the necessity of wholeness, of combining part with part. How much of this particular kind of reconciliation of opposites Williams got from others, notably Coleridge, and how much simply from an acute observation of the nature of things, we cannot know. But certainly this theme of joining haunts and, to a large degree, unifies the poem.

Let us now turn to the major problem. To what purpose is Charles Williams using the Arthurian myth? First of all, it should be apparent that the cycle as a whole deals with the unifying of Christianity and civilization, of spirit and flesh, of form and matter. Thus it is that throughout the poem we find on every level themes and images dealing with order and Exchange. It should also be apparent that this order is constantly frustrated by man's desire for self-sufficiency and independence. The main theme of the cycle thus becomes the battle between order and chaos, charity and cupidity, love and pride, Exchange and possession. Such a theme is, of course, universal, and there can be little doubt that Williams saw these battles in terms as relevant to twentieth-century London as to Arthurian Britain. Before going on with the general problem, however, let us look for a moment at Williams' novels in order to see how these major themes are reflected there, and to illustrate how Williams uses myth in the novels.

IV

The first thing that strikes one reading Williams' novels for the first time is his use of the occult and the mythical. The first five novels make great use of frankly mythological properties (in the stage sense) and of frankly supernatural or subnatural personages and events. The Holy Grail in *War in Heaven* (1930), a stone from Suleiman's crown in *Many Dimensions* (1931), the personifications of archetypes in *The Place of the Lion* (1931), the Tarot deck in *The Greater Trumps* (1932), and the diabolical Nigel Considine and the pagan revolt in *Shadows of Ecstasy* (1931)—all of these furnish for Williams convenient and striking means of introducing the particular themes of good and evil, order and chaos, which he is attempting to express. In each case, we have almost the same technique. Williams forces an occurrence of tremendous cosmic significance into modern society and then settles back to watch its effects on ordinary human beings. Moreover, the intrusion of these cosmic phenomena generally results in an overthrowing of natural order that can only be restored by the actions of the hero. Thus, in *The Greater Trumps*, when Henry attempts to use the Tarot deck for murder, a world-destroying storm is unleashed which can be quelled only by Nancy's effort to restore the missing, and thus dangerous, cards. Again, in *The Place of the Lion*, the sudden appearance of personified animal archetypes brings about chaos and destruction until Anthony, by himself becoming the archetype Man, names and so orders the beasts. But in each case, the miraculous is used only as a primer to set off the human reactions of the characters to these abnormal intrusions into their lives. In *War in Heaven,* for example, the sudden appearance of the Grail in England is not tremendously important in itself; its significance lies in the fact that it gives a focus to Gregory Persimmon's desire for supernatural power, Kenneth Mornington's romanticism, the Duke of North Riding's love of family and Church tradition, and the Archdeacon of Fardles' selflessness. In *Many Dimensions,* the discovery of the miraculous stone from Suleiman's crown is chiefly important in that it brings to the surface the fanaticism of Prince Ali Mirza Khan, the scientific zeal of Sir Giles, the greed of Reginald, the humane justice of Lord Arglay, and the selfless humility of Chloe Burnett. The focus of interest in the novels is always on the earthly characters themselves and on their reactions to the sudden revelation of the supernatural forces that surround them. Thus Williams' novels are far from being simply supernatural adventure stories. They are in the first instance novels about morality and religion among men.

The heroes and heroines, moreover, of Williams' novels are generally passive in the midst of the universe-shaking events that reveal the latent good and evil tendencies of the lesser characters. In each of the novels, those who covet the miraculous objects for their personal use, whether for good or for evil purposes, are branded as partially evil by Williams since these persons seek to make personal that which is universal and thus in essence unpossessable. For example, in *Many Dimensions* Sir Giles wishes the stone of Suleiman so that he may experiment with it, Reginald wishes to sell it and its types as means of transportation, the Prince wishes to return it to his House, and the Mayor of Rich desires to use it to cure the sick of his village. Only Lord

Arglay's secretary, Chloe, desires that the stone should exist for its own sake. Again, only the Archdeacon of Fardles in *War in Heaven* is content to let the Grail act for itself; he desires merely to become the agency of the Grail's force, never to be its possessor for any purpose whatsoever. The other characters in the novel, Sir Giles, Gregory, Riding, Kenneth Mornington, and the Eastern Satanists all desire the Grail as means to their own ends. This apparent passivity, this giving up of oneself to the greater will, marks Williams' heroes and heroines. They all exist for something greater than themselves.

We can, I think, best observe Williams' use of myth in the novels by examining one of his later novels. *Descent into Hell*[24] is a good choice since, although it is not the last of the novels (*All Hallows' Eve* [1945] was published eight years later), it stands at the climax of Williams' most intensive period of novel writing and includes more of Williams' major themes than any other of his novels. Unfortunately, the one novel that deals with Arthurian matters, *War in Heaven*, is almost useless for our purposes since it contains no hint of the elaborate reconstruction of the Arthurian myth which Williams later developed.

The plot structure of *Descent into Hell* like that of most of Williams' novels is markedly complex. The action of this multileveled novel takes place on Battle Hill, an English village near London, Williams' "City," a village in which in past ages the blood of martyrs has been shed. Here also in time past a workman, frustrated by the fact that "all his life he had been the butt of . . . an unkind world" (*DIH* 26), had taken his own life. The Hill itself emerges as one of the characters of the novel; its influence, the accumulation of centuries of human experience, dominates and shapes the action. It is, as Stanhope, the poet-hero, remarks later, significant that the "plague" should have begun on Battle Hill since "the dead were very thick there" (*DIH* 212).

Descent into Hell deals frankly with the communion of living and dead, of body and spirit here at Battle Hill. A young girl, Pauline Anstruther, shy and sensitive, has for many years suffered the "black panic" of meeting herself, her *Doppelgänger,* "coming up the drive" (*DIH* 22). Another of the Hill's occupants, the poet Peter Stanhope, suggests that she transfer her fear of her double to him, that she take her place within the great chain of Exchange:

> "We all know what fear and trouble are. Very well—when you leave here you'll think to yourself that I've taken this particular trouble over instead of you. You'd do as much for me if I needed it, or for any one. And I will give myself to it. I'll think of what comes to you, and imagine it, and know it, and be afraid of it. (*DIH* 97)

Pauline accepts Stanhope's strange offer, and finds in her next encounter with the *Doppelgänger* that her fear has departed. Having accepted the law of Exchange, she is able to perform an act of kindness toward the dead workman who still wanders about the Hill searching for the City of Redemption; finally, by a great act of love, she takes upon herself the fear of a martyred ancestor and in an act of charity bridging centuries (since the co-inherence may be in time and in space) accomplishes a reconciliation with her mirrored self:

> She had her offer to make now and it would not be refused. She herself was offered, in a most certain fact, through four centuries, her place at the table of exchange. The moment of goodwill in which she had directed to the City the man who had but lately died had opened to her the City itself, the place of the present and all the past. He was afraid, this martyr of her house, and she knew what to do. (*DIH* 169)

Thus Pauline achieves salvation by the law of Exchange, by an operation of charity.

Running parallel with the story of Pauline's salvation

is the account of the self-destruction of Lawrence Wentworth, the historian of Battle Hill. Wentworth, cherishing a warped and futile desire for Adela Hunt, one of the villagers, creates out of his own lust a succubus, an image of Adela which he can control and which will respond to his affection. In direct opposition to Pauline who is saved through her sympathy and love for others, Wentworth, in rejecting his profession and all humanity, turns inwardly to self-love and descends finally into hell. Upon seeing the image of the suicide workman:

> He sprang forward and up, to drive it away, to curse it lest it interpolated its horrid need between himself and his perfection. He would not have it; no canvassers, no hawkers, no tramps. He shouted angrily, making gestures; it offended him; it belonged to the City, and he would not have a City —no City, no circulars, no beggars. No; no; no. No people but his, no loves but his. (*DIH* 88)

These two stories interlock to make up the main narrative pattern of the novel. Intertwined with them is the workman's search for the City and thus for salvation and the account of the journey of Pauline's aunt, Mrs. Anstruther, toward death.

In *Descent into Hell* we may see Williams working with myth. The actual process here in the novel, however, needs a few remarks that will serve to separate it from the process involved in the Arthurian poems. Generally, it seems to me that myth is used in the novels, particularly in *Descent into Hell,* to universalize what is basically a highly improbable and therefore highly specific fictional situation. There is certainly nothing common to the experience of all men in a young girl's saving a martyred ancestor from the fear of death, or in an elderly historian's self-made descent into hell. Thus, I fancy, Williams hits upon myth as a means of generalizing the specific problems of his characters. That Lawrence Wentworth keeps an unholy tryst with a self-made and obscene image of Adela Hunt means nothing in terms of the ordinary man's experience; when, however, Charles Williams labels Wentworth's situation as Gomorrah and his hell-born mistress as Lilith, he embraces another layer of meaning through myth used as metaphor and so involves the reader in what is a generally accepted, and thus universal, level of experience. Myth in the novel thus becomes a medium of approach by which a modern situation is given depth in time and in universality and so gains in weight and significance. In the poetry, the situation is reversed. Instead of starting with a specifically contemporary, though frankly supernatural, situation and leading through that situation to the mythical patterns that make it universal, Williams begins with the terms of the myth itself and ascribes to it a broad pattern of meaning designed to enlarge our understanding of the contemporary world. The effects of the latter system we shall observe presently; the effect in the novel is to create and maintain simultaneously multiple levels of meaning and thus to universalize the theme of the novel.

Battle Hill, in *Descent into Hell,* is on one occasion significantly compared to the human body:

> He [Wentworth] lay quiet; beyond heart and lungs he had come, in the depth of the Hill, to the bottom of the body. He saw before him, in the disappearing moonlight, a place of cisterns and broad tanks, on the watery surface of which the moon still shone and from which a faint mist still arose. Between them, covering acres of ground, an enormous shape lay, something like a man's; it lay on its face, its shoulders and buttocks rose in mounds, and the head beyond; he could not see the legs lower than the thighs, for that was where he himself lay, and they could not be seen, for they were his own. He and the Adam sprang from one source; high over him he felt his heart

beat and his lungs draw breath. His machinery operated, far away. . . .

The Adam slept; the mist rose from the ground. The son of Adam waited. (*DIH* 87–88)

The body of Battle Hill is that of Adam; the tempting of Wentworth becomes metaphorically the battle of the Fall.

Again, in a chapter called "Return to Eden," the image of Adela first approaches Wentworth, leading him downward into the bowels of Battle Hill with the comforting words, comforting at least to Wentworth, that he does not "think enough about himself" (*DIH* 82). The specter leads him through a wooden door (later to be identified with the door of the graveyard hut where Lily Sammile lives) and down, symbolically, into his own body:

The darkness was quiet; his heart ceased to burn, though he could hear its beating, in time with the lapping and lulling waters. He had never heard his heart beating so loudly; almost as if he were inside his own body, listening to it there. . . .

They stopped. In the faint green light, light of a forest, faint mist in a forest, a river-mist creeping among the trees, moon in the mist, he could just see the shape of the woman beside him. He might be back again in Eden, and she be Eve. . . .

She was saying, eagerly: "Yes, yes, yes: better than Eve, dearer than Eve, closer than Eve. It's good for man to be alone. Come along, come along: farther in, farther in: down under, down under." . . .

She whose origin is with man's, kindred to him as he to his beasts, alien from him as he from his beasts; to whom a name was given in a myth, Lilith for a name and Eden for a myth. . . . (*DIH* 84–89)

Thus, Adam-Wentworth chooses the unreal, the selfish (Adela-Lilith) instead of the real, the companionate

(Adela-Eve). On one level Wentworth's descent into hell becomes an image of the progress of all hell-bound men. It is significant, here as elsewhere, that Williams makes no attempt at sustained allegory. Thus, my designation of the real Adela as the mythical Eve is not precisely correct; Williams nowhere admits the equation. Yet the reader, working out of the identification of the specter Adela–Lily Sammile image and the Wentworth-Adam image, is here almost forced to identify the real Adela as a potential Eve, even though later in the novel Adela herself is wrecked and desires the company of Lily. In short, we are not dealing with a novel that can be systematically interpreted on a number of levels throughout. It is enough for Williams' purposes here to suggest, and he really does no more than suggest, that the story of Wentworth's fall is that of the Fall of Man since the basic sin involved—pride, self-sufficiency—is the same. Thus, myth in Williams' novels may be said to suggest universal patterns rather than to delineate them.

The image of Gomorrah is associated with Wentworth throughout the novel. Stanhope explains it:

"The Lord's glory fell on the cities of the plain, of Sodom and another. We know all about Sodom nowadays, but perhaps we know the other even better. Men can be in love with men, and women with women, and still be in love and make sounds and speeches, but don't you know how quiet the streets of Gomorrah are? haven't you seen the pools that everlastingly reflect the faces of those who walk with their own phantasms, but the phantasms aren't reflected, and can't be. . . . There's no distinction between lover and beloved; they beget themselves on their adoration of themselves, and they live and feed and starve on themselves, and by themselves too, for creation, as my predecessor said, is the mercy of God, and they won't have the facts of creation." (*DIH* 174)

Sodom becomes simple homosexuality, "men in love with men, and women with women." But even this to Williams is love, sterile love, yes, but at least possessing passion and need of others. Gomorrah is the sort of spiritual incest which Wentworth practices—to fall in love with one's own creation, to adore a specter created from one's own lust, depending on nothing outside oneself, existing for none save oneself. It is the consummation of evil, the turning inward of all desire until the real world falls away. It is "Gomorrah in the Plain, illusion and the end of illusion; the opposite of holy fact, and the contradiction of sacred love" (*DIH* 203). The image of Gomorrah like that of Adam and Lilith serves to make plain, I think, the fact that Williams' theme is applicable not simply to the strange events of Battle Hill, but to mankind generally; Battle Hill is a particular place and Wentworth a particular man; Gomorrah is at once a condition and a judgment of that condition.

Goodness as well as evil is made universal by myth in *Descent into Hell*. It is clear that the substitution that is the center of the novel is a type of the Incarnation and Atonement:

> There, rooted in the heart of the Church at its freshest, was the same strong thrust of interchange. Bear for others; be baptized for others; and, rising as her new vision of the world had done once and again, an even more fiery mystery of exchange rolled through her horizons, turning and glancing on her like the eyed and winged wheels of the prophet. The central mystery of Christendom, the terrible fundamental substitution on which so much learning had been spent and about which so much blood had been shed, showed not as a miraculous exception, but as the root of a universal rule . . . "behold, I shew you a mystery," as supernatural as that Sacrifice, as natural as carrying a bag. (*DIH* 188–189)

This action of giving and receiving implies coöperation with humanity; it stands opposed to the selfishness of the inhabitants of Gomorrah. Substitution is, as Williams says, the "heart of the Church" and, as such, becomes a matter of universal concern. The reference in the passage quoted to the Christian doctrine of the Incarnation serves as do other references to mythology to give the rather odd spectacle of a young poet's assuming a girl's fear a universal significance that becomes understandable only in terms of the myth to which it is referred. Thus, to Williams, the process that lies behind the Incarnation is repeated over and over again in the history of mankind. It need not even be spoken of; it is a matter of tacit consent, a problem of common courtesy. The apparently strange illustration of the doctrine in *Descent into Hell* is simply an extension of what is, in reality, an everyday occurrence, a "universal rule." So again, the mythological reference in the novel renders the particular universal and the mystifying ordinary.

Let us return again to the poetry and for the moment apply T. S. Eliot's theory of poetic composition to the situation. Eliot believes that the only way of expressing emotion in the form of art is by finding an "objective correlative; in other words, a set of objects, a situation, a chain of events which shall be the formula of that *particular* emotion. . . ."[25] Thus, the problem of the artist is that of finding in nature a set of terms, a myth in fact, which can carry and convey adequately to the reader his particular, though generalized, attitude toward the world.

Although it is exceedingly dangerous to generalize about the creative imagination, one thing seems clear. During the middle years of the 1930's, Williams' novels came more and more to deal with the problems of salvation and damnation in the contemporary world. The early thrillers, though important in showing the development of Williams' themes, generally treat good and evil as absolutes. Those who are condemned are condemned because they worship evil and despise good. Although the situations in these early novels reflect, as they are certainly intended to do, perfectly valid and meaningful theological and mystical states, they have not the general charity-cupidity theme that dominates the later novels and the poetry. The shift, I think, in Williams' writing during the 1930's is away from mystical vision and adventure and toward an attempt to picture salvation and damnation as they exist among the people of Williams' own time. What we find is an attempt to translate the kinds of mystical experience found in the early novels into less overtly fantastic literary situations. Thus, in *Descent into Hell* and *All Hallows' Eve,* there is a great deal less of the science fiction point of view that makes use of supernatural devices and props. But even in these novels, we still find an insistence on a mystical point of view that involves a frank intermingling of nature and supernature; the living and the dead associate, ordinary temporal bonds are broken, and the characters, under quite ordinary circumstances, indulge in mystical experiences without apology or pseudoscientific explanation.

How much the muddled affairs of Europe during this period affected Williams' development it is impossible to say. However, the background of war is certainly present in the last two novels. Battle Hill, the scene of death and martyrdom, assumes a good deal of importance in *Descent into Hell.* The two dead girls of *All Hallows' Eve* are killed in a postwar plane crash, and it is clear that the war background here does much to intensify the problems of good and evil as they exist in the novel. Certainly, also, the final poems of the Arthurian cycle deal, as of course they must, with war and chaos, but the threat of war and destruction pervades the whole cycle to a greater extent than it does in any of Williams' sources. What seems to have happened is that the threat of war in Europe increased the intensity of Williams' vision of the battle of good and evil involved in the Arthurian destruction. Thus, toward the middle of the 1930's we find Williams altering his approach to his major theme by using more ordinary, commonplace situations and, at the same time, by seeing and so intensifying his vision of good and evil in terms of war and bloodshed.

Taliessin through Logres (1938) was published during this period. It is impossible to say how Williams happened to hit upon the Arthurian legends as an objective correlative to his major themes. Certainly his early Arthurian poems, published in 1930 and 1931, contain only the merest "intimations of spirituality."[26] It is possible to say, however, what Williams saw in the legend, and particularly in the Grail quest, since it provided him with a setting that was at once fairy and religious. If my assumptions concerning Williams' creative processes and development are correct, it must have become increasingly apparent to Williams that it was impossible for him to translate completely his major themes into ordinary contemporary circumstances since by their very nature many of these themes were semi-mystical. Consider, for example, the doctrine of Exchange, which in essence is an extension of the Incarnation and Atonement to all human intercourse. Although this theme is treated as matter-of-factly as possible in *Descent into Hell,* it is clear that its very presence gives the novel a semimystical atmosphere that, while not out of place, is considerably removed from the ordinary life with which the novel deals. It may well be, of course, that Williams' plan in *Descent into Hell* is to produce just this mixture of the miraculous and the ordinary, but, on the other hand, the mystical nature of the theme is better suited to a setting in which it can operate normally and upon its own terms. Thus, by adopting as objective correlative a myth that has as a part of its normal construction just these mystical and semimagical qualities—the Grail, Merlin, the prophets—Wil-

liams could very well let his own mystical concepts—
the doctrines of Exchange, Beatrician love, Gomorrah—
function on their own proper levels without having to
force them into normal, everyday life situations to
which they are by nature alien.

Second, in the Arthurian materials, Williams found a
myth that could carry, without undue forcing, his
primary theme of order and chaos. In Malory he found
the story of the rise and fall of a would-be perfect
civilization. Moreover, the key to a religious interpretation of that fall lay to his hand in the failure of the Grail
quest. The theme of spiritual incest (Gomorrah) could
be presented by Arthur's conceiving Mordred on
Morgause. The practice of Exchange could be presented
as the guiding law of the perfect civilization. The Fall
of Man could be seen in the Dolorous Blow. On every
level, the legend could carry Williams' themes. I do
not mean to say that Williams simply read Malory and
immediately conceived the whole plan. Undoubtedly
many of the major themes of the poem were developed
and realized fully during the twenty-year process of
reshaping the old material. But since nearly all the
major themes of the poem appear in earlier works, it
seems safe to say that Williams became increasingly
aware of the potentialities of the Arthurian myth during
the middle 1930's and set about actually recreating it
during this period as a vehicle for themes that he had
already exploited.[27]

All this is, of course, hypothetical. It may very well
be that Williams first conceived these themes in terms
of the Arthurian myth. However, it seems reasonable
to assume that, although the causes for his turning to the
myth in the middle 1930's may not be as cut and dried
as I have intimated, the major themes nevertheless did
exist in Williams' mind before he saw in the myth an
opportunity to exploit his entire concept of Christian
life in mythopoetic terms.

To carry the argument a step further, *The Figure of Arthur* may reflect this process in action. Here we see Williams retracing the development of the Arthurian myth, pointing out at every step the hints, the suggestions that he planned to develop in terms of his own world view. Thus, when Williams sees the figure of the wounded Pelles guarding the Grail, he sees it in terms of the Fall and Redemption. Again, when he comes to deal with the courtly love material, he must convert that material to his own notion of chastity and love. The whole of *The Figure of Arthur* can be seen in this light as Williams' documentation of and commentary on his own creative process.

However, we have not as yet shown what the myth accomplishes, or why, in the final analysis, Williams chose a myth as vehicle. We have yet suggested only a partial answer—that the Arthurian myth was adaptable to Williams' world view. To decide why Williams uses myth takes us back into speculative material, but at this point, Williams himself furnishes us with a hint. In the poem "Taliessin's Song of the Unicorn," Williams makes certain assumptions about the nature of myth.

> Shouldering shapes of the skies of Broceliande
>   are rumours in the flesh of Caucasia; they raid
>   the west,
>   clattering with shining hooves, in myth scanned—
>   centaur, gryphon, but lordlier for verse is the
>   crest
>   of the unicorn, the quick panting unicorn. . . .
>   (*TTL* 22)

Lewis interprets this poem as an exposition of Williams' notion of the sanctified and celibate poet, the unicorn, the "cuckold of the wood," being the poet. On another level, however, the poem can be seen as a description of the mythopoetic process. Myths, "shapes of Broceliande," exist in reality within that sacred forest but become "rumours" in the natural world. The virgin, to

97

whom the unicorn is traditionally attracted, generally
scorns him and prefers the "true man," the "gay hunter."
But yet:

> . . . if any, having the cunning to call the grand
>> beast,
>> the animal which is but a shade till it starts to
>>> run,
>> should dare set palms on the point, twisting from
>>> the least
>> to feel the sharper impress, for the thrust to stun
> her arteries into channels of tears beyond blood
>> (O twy-fount, crystal in crimson, of the Word's
>>> side). . . . (TTL 22)

then might she become the "Mother of the Unicorn's
Voice" and her son the "new sound that goes / surrounding the City's reach." On one level, the girl may
very well be a type of the artist who, in bleeding and
suffering, may become a part of the myth itself (the
unicorn) and so produce a work of art, a "new sound
surrounding the City's reach."

The poem as a whole is, of course, a type of Williams'
constant longing for a "twy-nature," a joining and reconciliation that can produce a new whole, seen here
in an allusion to Christ, "crystal in crimson, of the
Word's side." But the identification of myth with an
ultimate reality that becomes a "rumour" in the "flesh
of Caucasia" seems to me to define part of Williams'
attitude toward myth and toward the creative operation. Consider a statement of Lewis' on the subject of
myth, the substance of which is remarkably close to
that of Williams' poem.

> My present view . . . would be that just as, on
> the factual side, a long preparation culminates in
> God's becoming incarnate as Man, so, on the doc-
> umentary side, the truth first appears in *mythical*
> form and then by a long process of condensing or
> focussing finally becomes incarnate as History.
> This involves the belief that Myth in general is

. . . a real though unfocussed gleam of divine
truth falling on human imagination.[28]

This I take to be Williams' attitude also; myth is un-
created, though rumored reality, reality that has not
yet become "incarnate as History," but reality nevertheless. Thus, to apply the generalization, the myth of
Arthur's kingdom is as real and thus as important and
as functional as that of modern England. The problem
of the artist is the same in each case. He must suffer
"intellectual nuptials" with the myth and make of his
stone and the myth's shell a new twy-natured work of
art, in which the old metaphor and the new meaning,
the old form and the new content join in a new creation.
In short, we have another reconciliation in artistic
creation.

If this is true, then at least a part of the problem is
solved. In Williams' mind, the danger of noncommuni-
cation with the reader is not incurred by a creative
process that places a contemporary theme in an antique
and essentially fairy-tale vehicle. If the metaphor is,
of itself (to rephrase Eliot's criticism of *Hamlet*), suf-
ficiently wide and strong enough to carry the burden
of the theme, then presumably any metaphor will do.
Thus, the writers of the Middle Ages could perfectly
well explain sin and salvation in terms of real or imagined animal characteristics and Swift can easily
condemn eighteenth-century social and political im-
perfections in terms of little men and giants. My contention, then, is this: the metaphor of contemporary
England could not hold Williams' theme; the metaphor
of Arthurian Logres could. *Ergo,* Taliessin goes through
Logres rather than London.

What Williams finds then in the Arthurian myth is a
mythopoetic vehicle that will serve to give full and
ordered expression to his conception of the relationship
of civilization and religion. The Arthurian myth, in
Williams' reading, gives order and symmetry to his
world view to an extent and with a completeness im-

possible in a contemporary metaphor. The long-range view with which a modern writer can look at myth partly accounts for this. The modern world in its proximity is chaotic and disorganized; the writer must see it in metaphorical terms in order to arrange it and thus, in some measure, control and interpret it. Myth "attempts to *underpin* the chaos of experience so that it may reveal the features of a structure—order, coherence, and meaning."[29] Thus, Williams' problems and themes begin as attitudes toward the modern world, but find their expression in myth.

I have already said that Williams uses myth referentially in the novels to render universal his specific and generally bizarre fictional situations. That is, in the novels Williams' method is to begin with the modern situation and then to extend his meaning through allusions to myth. In the poetry, on the other hand, we find Williams beginning and staying within the myth itself. At times, to be sure, he uses the method of the novels by making brief references to Christ ("crystal in crimson, of the Word's side") and in the partial identification of Galahad with Christ, but these references certainly do not constitute any pattern of allusion. Nor does Williams ever point forward by allusion as does Tennyson (one thinks immediately of the introductory verses to "Morte d'Arthur") to delineate the contemporary referent of the myth. Rather I think, Williams presents the Arthurian myth in apparent isolation, so that the whole myth may be seen in application to the contemporary world rather than single parts of it. Thus, we cannot go through Williams' reconstruction of the Arthurian myth and make point-by-point identifications along the way; we cannot say that Arthur is twentieth-century "this" or Lancelot twentieth-century "that." What we can do, however, is to view the whole myth as a general and symptomatic treatment of the modern situation. Thus, the general problems of sin and failure in the Arthurian cycle become symbolic representatives of our own modern problems as Williams sees them. The themes of the remade myth are applicable to, but never identifiable with specifically modern themes. Thus, myth is not used to generalize a specific situation but, conversely, is made to render specific a universal theme. We see the hope and failure of Logres as a whole; we see our contemporary Grail quest in fragments. To Williams' mythmaking mind, however, one thing is clear: both quests are failures. The hope in both cases exists in the company, the remnant, those to whom the doctrine of Exchange has operative validity. In the novels, this theme is often obscured by the fact that the chosen objective correlative cannot bear its weight. In the poetry, the theme takes on new meaning and new grandeur from the meaning and grandeur inherent in the myth itself.

4

C. S. Lewis

THE REPUTATION of C. S. Lewis depends to a large
extent on his prominence as a popular Christian apol-
ogist; he has become famous as a modern-day "apostle
to the skeptics." His theological writings are designed
for and directed toward skeptical laymen who have
been, in Lewis' opinion, unduly influenced by nine-
teenth-century liberalism and scientism and so have left
the Church and its fixed moral code for the greener
pastures of "humane science" and moral relativism.

Lewis' approach in books such as *The Screwtape
Letters, Mere Christianity,* and *The Problem of Pain* is
beautifully suited to his chosen task; he discusses the
weightiest of spiritual matters with the air of a cocktail-
party companion.

> Now on the face of it that [the Atonement] is a
> very silly theory. If God was prepared to let us
> off, why on earth did He not do so? And what
> possible point could there be in punishing an in-
> nocent person instead? . . . On the other hand,
> if you think of a debt, there is plenty of point in a
> person who has some assets paying it on behalf
> of someone who has not. . . . It is a matter of
> common experience that, when one person has got
> himself into a hole, the trouble of getting him out
> usually falls on a kind friend.[1]

The urbanity and wit of all of Lewis' polemical books are perhaps necessary. He is addressing an audience reared on Marx, Freud, and the Higher Criticism, a hostile audience that can be dealt with only on its own naturalistic terms and in its accustomed language. His sentiments are themselves hardly those found acceptable, or even tolerable, by most modern readers. Rejecting all relative moral codes, Lewis defends a traditional and absolute morality based on unequivocal righteousness. For example, in those chapters of *Christian Behavior* which deal with problems of marriage and sexual relations, Lewis' veneer of chatty sophistication covers a hard core of orthodox Christian morality:

> They tell you sex has become a mess because it was hushed up. But for the last twenty years it had *not* been hushed up. It has been chattered about all day long. Yet it is still a mess. If hushing up had been the cause of the trouble, ventilation would have set it right.[2]
>
> There is no getting away from it: the Christian rule is, "Either marriage, with complete faithfulness to your partner, or else total abstinence."[3]

It is obvious that Lewis, in promoting a conception of marriage which involves honor, obedience, and fidelity, is proposing a moral system that is usually described in our day as "Victorian" and "old-fashioned." Yet the manner, the tone, the whole approach in these books are as patently "modern" as a newspaper gossip column.

My point should be obvious. The deliberate stylishness of Lewis' theological works stems from his peculiar position as a modern defender of what is generally regarded as an outworn and stuffy Faith. He thus appears in these works as a cocktail-party *advocatus Christi* (we presumably no longer need an *advocatus diaboli*) attacking sophisticated skepticism with sophisticated Christianity, and moral relativism with ethical orthodoxy. We have before us in Lewis the spectacle of a man whose prose style is appealingly contemporary, upholding with great vigor and skill concepts that presumably went out of fashion with the great enlightenment of the flapper age. What Lewis is attempting is obvious, yet he is not merely sugar-coating the bitter pill of moral orthodoxy. In these books, Lewis is attempting to demonstrate, through style and method, that morality was never unpopular at all among the really clever people.

Lewis' writings (excepting, of course, *The Allegory of Love* and *English Literature in the Sixteenth Century*) are thus designed to woo mankind away from the laboratories and the secular reform movements and back again into the arms of the Church. Lewis in these books is a propagandist; his cause is Christian orthodoxy in religion and in morality; his methods are those of his enemies. His writings vary greatly; from *The Screwtape Letters* to *Miracles* is quite a journey. Yet no matter what the issue, the point of view remains constant. Lewis defends the old-fashioned emotions and decries those modern textbooks that attempt to subdue the "emotional reaction."[4] He defends physical pain and proclaims that fortitude is necessary for salvation.[5] He beats down the naturalists with their own logical clubs and then proceeds to defend the supernatural and the miraculous.[6] At all times, he views the world from the vantage point of the church steps.

Thus it is that when we approach Lewis' novels we should expect to find reflected there the same point of view, the same polished style, and the same general ideas that fill the theological writings. That is to say, Lewis' novels, with the exception of *Till We Have Faces,* deal exclusively with the orthodox conception of and approach to Christianity. There is no attempt in these novels, as there certainly is in the novels of Charles Williams, to work with a highly individualized, though nevertheless basically Christian, world view. As we have seen, Williams' Arthurian poems express in mythopoetic form concepts—for example, Beatrician love—which, though evolved from Christian doctrines, are nevertheless not a part of the usual Christian's interpretation of these doctrines. Lewis, on the other hand, promotes no such interpretations. His themes in the novels, like his statements in the theological books, are perfectly orthodox and traditional and are the common property of all Christians who accept the Faith and dogma of the Church.

That is not to say that Lewis is any less "creative" a writer than is Williams. Lewis, in fact, goes a step beyond Williams in one direction. Like Williams, he can reshape an older myth in order to provide himself with a suitable literary vehicle; but unlike Williams he at times creates his own myth.

Till We Have Faces demonstrates the first of these strategies; it is Lewis' reworking of the myth of Cupid and Psyche. The original story recounted how Cupid, sent by jealous Venus to harm the beautiful Psyche, fell in love with the girl and led her away to his mountain palace where he visited her at night, requiring only that she never attempt to look upon him. However, persuaded by her jealous sisters, Psyche looked upon the young god and was thereby doomed to live without him. After many trials, the lovers were united, and the story ends happily.

But Lewis' version of the myth is far from a simple retelling of the story. The conflict of faith and scientific rationalism, apparent in all of Lewis' work, emerges as the dominant theme of *Till We Have Faces,* and Lewis carefully reshapes the myth in order to emphasize this theme. The story in Lewis' novel is told by the princess Orual, one of Psyche's sisters. Orual has been thoroughly imbued by her Greek tutor with the spirit of rationalism and so does not believe in the local Aphrodite, a hideous, misshapen block of stone called Ungit. She cannot share her people's devotion to the goddess and so cannot accept or understand Psyche's new life in the palace of Cupid. She cannot (and this is the most significant of Lewis' changes in the myth) even *see* Cupid's palace, except in a brief moment of vision which she mistrusts and renounces. Thus Orual's plea to Psyche to look upon Cupid is not in Lewis' novel simply the act of a jealous sister; it is scientific enlightenment attempting to destroy faith. Psyche, of course, yields, but purely out of regard for her sister, who has threatened suicide, rather than from lack of faith. The rest of the novel presents in fictional terms the theme of Lewis' autobiography, *Surprised by Joy*—the search of Orual for what Lewis calls "joy" and the final capitulation of an honestly skeptical and questioning reason before the force of a God who will not answer the complaints of men, but who demands acceptance by faith and who by His power compels Orual to enter into belief.

In addition to this conflict of faith and reason, Lewis uses the Cupid-Psyche myth to introduce a doctrine of Exchange much like that of Charles Williams. By a remarkable transference, Orual in the course of the novel becomes both Ungit and Psyche. During the night of Psyche's treason, Cupid appears to Orual and announces to her that she "also shall be Psyche."[7] In the years following, Orual by unrelenting effort makes reason rather than superstition the rule of her government and of her state religion, but she is haunted always by a desire for Psyche and for something beyond her success. At last, in a vision, she realizes that she has become Ungit; like the goddess, in constantly demanding and using the talents and lives of her advisors, she has become "that all-devouring, womblike, yet barren, thing."[8] Her task, she realizes, is to accept the gods and with their aid to transform the ugly, demanding Ungit, whose temple reeks of blood sacrifice, into the shining Eros who had spoken to her on the mountain. She must, in short, herself—Ungit, Maia, the earth goddess —become the bride of Love.

This she does through Exchange. By taking upon herself the tasks imposed by Venus upon Psyche, by bearing the pain for another, Ungit is able to turn her selfish, devouring love into charity and so become in truth Psyche.

In *Till We Have Faces*, Lewis reshapes an old myth in order to make it a vehicle for his new theme. In his first three novels—*Out of the Silent Planet, Perelandra,* and *That Hideous Strength*—Lewis creates his own myth.[9] Science fiction provides him with a method and a plot, the theology of the Church with a theme.

A statement of the basis of Lewis' cosmic myth can be found in *A Case for Christianity*.

> Christianity agrees with Dualism that this universe is at war. But it does not think this is a war between independent powers. It thinks it is a civil war, a rebellion, and that we are living in a part of the universe occupied by the rebel.
>
> Enemy-occupied territory—that is what this world is. Christianity is the story of how the rightful king has landed, you might say landed in disguise, and is calling us all to take part in a great campaign of sabotage.[10]

In Lewis' first three novels, the earth becomes "Thulcandra," the "silent planet," cut off from the rest of the cosmos by the rebellion of Satan and subsequent Fall of Man. Elwin Ransom, the philologist-hero of Lewis' cycle, is kidnapped by Edward Weston, a physicist, and so is accidentally involved in a trip to Mars. There, upon meeting the Oyarsa, or planetary intelligence of that planet, he learns that the universe, apart from Earth, exists in harmony and peace, having a common language (Ransom's name for it is "Old Solar") and a common interplanetary religion and government.

It is clear that Lewis in describing this theocratic arrangement is seeking to translate the usual Christian concepts into pseudoscientific and mythical terms, without at the same time losing or distorting the basic

Christian ideas with which he is working. Thus, the two sets of terms involved can only approximate each other; the Martians, inhabiting as they do an unfallen world, cannot view Christianity from the same point of view as do fallen Earth men. For example, Lewis cannot in his novels permit the same kind of imprecision of diction as I have allowed myself in this last sentence. The term "Christianity," or even a strict Martian equivalent, would have no meaning to Martians who have never had need of a Redeemer. Moreover, having no need of the Holy Ghost since they have immediate grace, Martians have no conception of the Trinity. "Maleldil the Young," Ransom learns, first made the universe and now dwells with the "Old One." His nature is such, however, that he is not bound to dwell in any one particular place in the universe at any one time; "it became plain" to Ransom that Maleldil is a "spirit without body, parts or passions."[11] Thus, the Martians know the Father (the "Old One") as Maleldil (the Son). What Lewis would seem to be doing, therefore, in this description of God as He looks to a Martian is to incorporate into that description all the aspects of the Trinity which we on Earth normally see as separate qualities, but which the unfallen Martians see only in Maleldil. Presumably, to an inhabitant of Mars, there is no "Mystery" of the Trinity, no necessity of division by function, but rather an immediate perception of the whole essence of God.

This treatment of the Trinity represents the kind of problem that Lewis has to face throughout the novels. For example, how can he possibly account for the presence of evil on Mars where there has been no Fall? Again, Lewis' treatment of this problem corresponds to perfectly orthodox thinking on the problem of evil generally, but his presentation of the matter is, as it must be, given from a point of view differing radically from the usual approach that takes for its starting point the Fall of Man. On Mars, Ransom finds that there exist dangerous water beasts called "hneraki" (the singular form is "hnakra") who periodically attack those Martians (called "hrossa") who inhabit the low lands. Ransom asks why Maleldil created the "hnakra." Hyoi, a "hross," answers that the "forest would [not] be so bright, nor the water so warm, nor love so sweet, if there were no danger in the lakes" (SP 79). In short, Lewis is proposing here a perfectly orthodox, non-Manichean answer to the problem of the existence of evil. God allows evil to exist in the universe for reasons that man does not know, but which are eventually for man's good.

Lewis' main aim in the creation of his silent-planet myth is thus to create and maintain a metaphor that will serve to carry in fictional form the basic tenets of Christianity and present them from a non-Christian point of view but without reference to normal Christian symbols. The main tenor of Lewis' myth is Christian orthodoxy; his vehicle is science fiction. This general method is graphically illustrated in *Perelandra*, the second novel of the trilogy. Ransom, summoned by Maleldil through the Oyarsa of Mars, journeys to Perelandra (Venus). There he finds a young world, a Paradise. He meets the queen of that world, who tells him that Maleldil has forbidden that she and her husband should sleep on a certain fixed island (most of Venus' islands are floating). Weston, the physicist who originally kidnapped Ransom and transported him to Mars, now appears, but it is immediately apparent that Satan (the Bent Eldil) has taken possession of Weston's body in an attempt to tempt the queen to sleep on the forbidden island in order to bring about another Fall. The novel from this point on settles down into argumentation—Ransom, the emissary of Maleldil, seeks to preserve the queen's innocence; Weston, the devil incarnate, attempts to confound her with arguments glorifying the knowledge of evil.

It is apparent that Lewis is here expounding, from the

point of view of his own cosmic myth, the doctrine of the Fall of Man. The theological problem, as Lewis sees it, centers upon the validity of that interpretation that sees the Fall as fortunate. Weston himself introduces the doctrine, and Ransom must answer:

> "Whatever you do, He will make good of it. But not the good He had prepared for you if you had obeyed Him. That is lost for ever. The first King and first Mother of our world did the forbidden thing; and He brought good of it in the end. But what they did was not good; and what they lost we have not seen."[12]

The problem is seen again in one of Ransom's reveries: "'Other things, other blessings, other glories,' he murmured. . . . 'God can make good use of all that happens. But the loss is real'" (*PE* 158). Lewis' own opinion would seem to be indicated by these statements. The Fall on Earth was fortunate in that God, almost by definition, brings good out of evil. Yet had the Fall not occurred, some equally great good, forever lost to man, would have been revealed.

The main point to be made concerning the first two books of the trilogy is this: Lewis, using the literary methodology of the writers of science fiction, is attempting, as in his tracts dealing with Christian apologetics, to justify the ways of God to skeptical man by presenting the core of the Faith. His main appeal, as in the tracts, is directed toward the skeptic and the apostate. He must, however, describe and define the theological tenets with which he is dealing from a point of view that, of necessity, cannot make use of the normal terminology of the Church.

This is, of course, both a strength and a weakness. The old terms have the advantage of producing stock responses, which is one of the great advantages of literary allusion to known and accepted myth. Lewis himself occasionally takes advantage of this quality of myth although he is careful to keep within his own chosen point of view in doing it. For example, in *Perelandra*, Weston, the Un-man, suddenly

> threw back its head and cried in a voice so loud that it seemed the golden sky-roof must break, "*Eloi, Eloi, lama sabachthani.*"
> And the moment it had done so, Ransom felt certain that the sounds it had made were perfect Aramaic of the First Century. The Un-man was not quoting; it was remembering. (*PE* 159–160)

This passage reinforces the identification of Weston with Satan by an allusion to the Crucifixion. Its strength lies, of course, in the fact that it forces the reader to bring forward all his traditional responses to the Good Friday scene, and in doing so to share Ransom's horror.

Yet this calling forth of stock responses has serious disadvantages. The stock responses attached to usual Christian terms may very well repel the very people whom Lewis is trying hardest to reach. Thus it is that Lewis' seemingly non-Christian point of view in the novels is one of his chief sources of strength; it functions in the same way as did his sophisticated prose style in the theological books. In both cases, Lewis would seem to be working on the principle that the usual approach to Christianity is no longer effective, so that totally different terms must be used to express the old and, for Lewis, still valid doctrines.

In *That Hideous Strength*, the third of the novels, Lewis retains his general method in that he presents orthodox Christianity by means of non-Christian terms, but in this novel he shifts his emphasis to some extent away from the silent-planet myth developed in the first two novels. The primary structure of the myth is still retained: Ransom is still Lewis' hero; we have allusions to Weston, the physicist; the moon, as in the other novels, is Earth's battle perimeter. But the field of action shifts from heaven to earth. Hints thrown out in the first two novels that the great battle to rescue Earth was shortly to be begun are developed here. Ransom appears in this novel as a Mr. Fisher-King who maintains a household near the village of Edgestow and Bracton College; from this vantage point he wages war against the forces of the Bent Eldil, who is militantly setting out to capture England and the world. Evil takes the form of a sociological and scientific society whose professed aim is the amelioration of social and economic conditions by means of the creation of a secular coöperative state. Yet this society, ironically called the N.I.C.E. (National Institute of Coördinated Experiments), is in reality only a façade for the operations of the Bent Eldil, who is attempting to conquer the world by appealing to ideals of secular humanism, science, and progress:

> Man has got to take charge of Man. That means, remember, that some men have got to take charge of the rest. . . . [The N.I.C.E. has in mind] quite simple and obvious things, at first—sterilization of the unfit, liquidation of backward races . . . , selective breeding. Then real education, including pre-natal education.[13]

> It is the beginning of Man Immortal and Man ubiquitous. . . . Man on the throne of the universe. (*HS* 204)

Weston, we remember, in *Out of the Silent Planet* and *Perelandra* had held the same dreams that by Creative Evolution man would eventually triumph over the universe. And it is, of course, against precisely this same sort of secularism and skepticism that Lewis' arguments in the theological tracts are directed.

Mr. Fisher-King represents the power of Maleldil on earth; his travels have established for him a mode of communication with the outer universe. Yet it would seem that Lewis in *That Hideous Strength* deliberately deëmphasizes the silent-planet myth. The reason for such a decision seems obvious; Lewis' cosmic machinery cannot properly function in an "earth" story. He thus introduces another myth to take the place of the cosmic adventure story—the Arthurian myth.

Lewis abstracts from the Arthurian myth only those elements necessary to his purpose. The general assumption that underlies Lewis' use of the Arthurian myth is the popular tradition, which begins with Wace and Layamon, that Arthur was transported to the Isle of Avalon (usually associated with the Celtic Elysium), there to be cured of his wounds. According to the tradition, he stands perpetual guard over England and will return when he is needed. Lewis then envisions a perpetual dichotomy and conflict (first developed, I think, by Charles Williams) between Logres and Britain, the Arthurian ideal and the secular reality.

> . . . something we call Britain is always haunted by something we call Logres. Haven't you noticed that we are two countries? After every Arthur, a Mordred; behind every Milton, a Cromwell: a nation of poets, a nation of shopkeepers; the home of Sidney—and of Cecil Rhodes. (*HS* 441–442)

Both Mr. Fisher-King, the representative of Logres, and the N.I.C.E., which constitutes modern Britain, are attempting to find the body of the magician Merlin, who, according to tradition, did not die but was cast into a deep sleep by Nimue; both sides wish to make use of Merlin's magical power to achieve their ends.

From the Grail myth Lewis takes the figure of the wounded Fisher King, who in *That Hideous Strength* is half-human, half-divine. Upon seeing Mr. Fisher-King for the first time, Jane Studdock, the heroine of the novel, is struck by his apparent youthfulness, and his seeming agelessness throughout the book does much to establish his position as an almost mythological character:

> It came over her, with a sensation of quick fear, that this face was of no age at all. She had . . . disliked bearded faces except for old men with white hair. But that was because she had long

113

since forgotten the imagined Arthur of her child-
hood—and the imagined Solomon too. . . . For
the first time in all those years she tasted the
word *King* itself with all its linked associations of
battle, marriage, priesthood, mercy, and power.
(*HS* 160)

Ransom, we discover later, is not only the Fisher King
of the Arthurian legend; he is also the Pendragon, and
his household is the remnant of Logres:

Ransom was summoned to the bedside of an old
man then dying in Cumberland. . . . That man
was the Pendragon, the successor of Arthur and
Uther and Cassibelaun. Then we learned the truth.
There has been a secret Logres in the very heart of
Britain all these years; an unbroken succession of
Pendragons. (*HS* 442)

Somewhat later we find the reason that Bracton College
and Edgestow are the principal battlegrounds of the
two forces. We find that:

. . . Edgestow lay in what had been the very
heart of ancient Logres, that the village of Cure
Hardy preserved the name of Ozana le Coeur
Hardi, and that a historical Merlin had once
worked in what was now Bracton Wood. . . .
Merlin had not died. His life had been hidden,
sidetracked . . . for fifteen centuries. But under
certain conditions it would return to his body.
(*HS* 231, 233)

These elements, then—the perpetual battle between
Logres and Britain; the reappearance of Ransom as
the Fisher King and the Pendragon; the remnant of
Logres; and the figure of Merlin—constitute the core of
the Arthurian story as Lewis uses it in *That Hideous
Strength*. What Lewis seems to see in the Arthurian
myth is a metaphor that will fit within the over-all
scheme of the silent-planet myth and at the same time
reinforce his general scheme by expressing it in yet
another and more overtly literary set of terms. Thus,

the Arthurian material in a sense can be said to exist both within the silent-planet myth and parallel to it. Since I have already pointed out the ways in which Lewis establishes continuity with the rest of the series, I shall turn directly to a discussion of the ways in which the Arthurian myth, as Lewis uses it, parallels the silent-planet myth of Lewis' own making.

It is evident that Lewis in emphasizing the eternal war between Logres and Britain is attempting to develop a symbol that will parallel roughly the war between good and evil forces on Earth, the silent planet. Just as in the other novels he has carefully delineated the position of Earth as "enemy-held territory," so here he is expressing the same concept in other terms. Logres is the "haunting . . . from the other side of the invisible wall" (*HS* 441), from behind the moon's orbit, from Deep Heaven. Logres is represented in British history by Arthur, Milton, Sidney, Britain by Mordred, Cromwell, Rhodes. Britain forever attempts to destroy what Logres builds. Obviously, both in this novel and in Lewis' over-all myth, Britain is the more powerful of the two; the bent eldila outnumber the good on the silent planet. Yet, in Lewis' terms, Logres still haunts, though it never quite (at least, as yet) wins. It seems evident to me that this contest of Logres and Britain comes to Lewis directly from the poetry of Charles Williams rather than from the usual Arthurian sources. There it is seen in the contrast between Bors and Kay, between those who practice "many a turn of exchange" and those "wise in economics." But it also seems evident to me that Lewis has succeeded in fitting this material perfectly to his already established myth and pattern. This he does by stating that what we call the Arthurian "myth" is a record of historical fact and by asserting that the history of the struggle between Logres and Britain has never been described in its proper terms.

When the history of these last few months comes to be written in *your* [McPhee the skeptic's] lan-

guage, and printed, and taught in schools, there
will be no mention in it of you and me, nor of Merlin and the Pendragon and the Planets. And yet in
these months Britain rebelled most dangerously
against Logres and was defeated only just in time.

(HS 442)

Thus, Lewis is free to introduce a real Merlin and a real
Fisher King and allow them to function as historical personages in the novel without violating the definition of
fictional reality which he himself has made. The de-
scriptions of the working of N.I.C.E., on the other hand,
are too faithful to the actual contemporary scene to
need fictional justification. Having then established the
reality of his conflict, Lewis can link it to his over-all
pattern of the silent-planet myth (1) by keeping Ransom
and the eldila as characters and (2) by showing that
the fight between Logres and Britain in the Arthurian
myth is, in fact, a manifestation, a microcosm of the
universal conflict, the war in heaven which he had discussed in the first two novels. Again, the temptations
that the N.I.C.E. bring forward are remarkably similar
in tone, method, and purpose to those used by Satan in
Perelandra and to those Williams attributes to Mordred
in his Arthurian poetry—the temptation to worship the
self, the state, the beloved for itself; it is, again, *cupiditas* as opposed to *caritas*.

In the personage of Mr. Fisher-King, Lewis has por-
trayed a new and almost divine Ransom, now an in-
heritor of the guardianship of the Grail and thus the
head of the new Logres. Perhaps the most significant
detail that Lewis uses in his description of Mr. Fisher-
King is the bleeding foot, the result, in terms of the silent-planet myth, of the physical struggle with Weston-
Satan in *Perelandra*. On this level, the wound is made
a symbol of Ransom's fallen state; it is the sting of the
serpent ("thou shalt bruise his heel"). The wounded
heel also suggests, of course, the vulnerable heel of
Achilles which in that myth also functions as a symbol

of the hero's humanity, an inheritance from his father. But this wound functions equally well when seen as a part of the Fisher King myth. The Fisher King suffers from the "dolorous stroke" of Balin the Savage, an ever-bleeding wound in the thigh. According to Charles Williams' interpretation of the myth, which I think we can presume Lewis accepted, this blow becomes a symbol of the Fall, an indication that the earth has been made a waste land and can be made fertile only by the touch of the sanctity that the Grail represents. The symbol of the wound would seem to be remarkably similar in function in both myths, and it is the common qualities of the symbol which Lewis is attempting to exploit. The wounded heel becomes a symbol of Mr. Fisher-King's heritage both as a keeper of the Grail and as a man among men, and by transferring the wound from thigh to heel, Lewis involves both myths. The wound becomes, by extension, a symbol of the waste land of modern society, land laid waste by the victory of the Bent Eldil and incurable until Logres captures Britain and the battle line of the moon's orbit is broken. Then, we presume, the wound that must be present even in the most perfect of men can be healed. The purposes of Logres and the dream of the eldila of Deep Heaven are thus identified through the symbol of the wounded Mr. Fisher-King, who happens also to be the space traveler, Elwin Ransom. Thus are the myths made parallel.

The identification of Ransom–Fisher King with the Pendragon can also be said to extend the implications of Lewis' theme. Lewis views the Arthurian myth from Williams' vantage point; thus, he thinks of Arthurian Britain as the ideal secular civilization awaiting a reconciliation with its religious counterpart. By making the triple identification, Ransom–Fisher King–Pendragon, Lewis completes Williams' pattern by joining the Grail (Mr. Fisher-King) with the ideal kingdom (the Pendragon) with Deep Heaven (Ransom the voyager).

The menage of Mr. Fisher-King represents, within the novel, a microcosm of the Arthurian court; it bears a very decided resemblance to Williams' "Company of Taliessin," and in fact is referred to as a "company" within this novel (HS 126). The household kept by Mr. Fisher-King is made up for the most part of perfectly ordinary people who are united in their common cause and by their common devotion to Mr. Fisher-King. They are primarily characterized by kindness and generosity, and, because of these qualities, function as an amiable and civilized group. Lewis dwells on the idyllic and co-operative aspects of the civilization represented by the company at St. Anne's in order to provide a contrast with the secular civilization (if it can be called that) represented by the Belbury headquarters of N.I.C.E. This latter group lacks leadership and a clear-cut cause. No one at Belbury is quite sure of his exact place in the organization; no one is quite sure to whom he is responsible. The organization is split by jealousies and factional strife. In short, Belbury would seem to represent the chaotic society founded on *cupiditas* rather than upon *caritas*. Mr. Fisher-King's household, on the other hand, is based upon the working ideals of hierarchy (all owe allegiance to Mr. Fisher-King) and communal effort (all share the menial household tasks). The organization at St. Anne's would seem to proceed on the very principle Williams demanded but found lacking in the Arthurian court. Ransom, addressing the group, says:

> "Do you think I would claim the authority I do if the relation between us depended either on your choice or mine? You never chose me. I never chose you. . . . You and I have not started or devised this; it has descended on us—sucked us into itself, if you like. It is, no doubt, an organisation; but we are not the organisers." (HS 229)

What seems to be implied here is that Mr. Fisher-King

118

and the members of the company exist for the sake of the company, not the company for them. This is, of course, the correct relationship of individual and state according to Williams; the king exists for the kingdom, not the kingdom for the king.

That Lewis means this contrast of St. Anne's and Belbury to be taken seriously is seen in the fact that he provides a point of comparison by which we may judge the groups by similar standards. Both households keep animals and in the treatment of those animals by each group we are intended to see their basic dissimilarity. At Belbury, the animals are caged awaiting vivisection; at St. Anne's they are treated as "jesters, servants, and playfellows" (*HS* 453). In short, the society at St. Anne's is linked through the personage of the Pendragon with the ideal and ordered society of the Arthurian court.

Lewis' introduction of Merlin is the last of his major interpolations of Arthurian materials. Merlin, as I have said, is the key figure of the novel. Both sides desire the "mantle of Merlin," the supernatural power that the great magician represents. In Lewis' characterization, Merlin is seen as a representative of the power of nature. He

> is the reverse of Belbury. He's at the opposite extreme. He is the last vestige of an old order in which matter and spirit were, from our modern point of view, confused. For him every operation on Nature is a kind of personal contact, like coaxing a child or stroking one's horse. After him came the modern man to whom Nature is something dead. . . . (*HS* 336)

He offers to cure Ransom's wound:

> "Sir," said Merlinus, in a deeper and softer voice, "I could take all the anguish from your heel as though I were wiping it out with a sponge. Give me but seven days to go in and out and up and

down and to and fro, to renew old acquaintance. These fields and I, this wood and I, have much to say to one another." (HS 338)

Merlin is seen also as a gigantic anachronism, a man of the Arthurian world transported to an environment he does not understand. Dimble says:

"We'd the dickens of a job to make him understand that Ransom isn't the king of this country or trying to become king. And then we had to break it to him that we weren't the British at all, but the English—what he'd call Saxons. It took him some time to get over that." (HS 332)

Merlin constantly complains about the customs of the country in which he finds himself and, in one scene, insists on driving on the old and familiar Roman road although it leads him directly through grass and ruts.

Merlin, in his strange and comic animality and other-worldliness, would seem at first glance to be used by Lewis only as a bit of inorganic particularity designed to delight the reader. But as Ransom explains his own history to Merlin, the true function of the magician becomes apparent. The powers of Maleldil will work only through

". . . a man whose mind is open to be . . . invaded, . . . one who by his own will once opened it. . . . And through a black magician's mind their purity neither can nor will operate. One who has dabbled . . . in the days when dabbling had not begun to be evil, or was only just beginning . . . and also a Christian man and a penitent. . . . In all these Western parts of the world there was only one man who had lived in those days and could still be recalled. You—" (HS 343)

During the terrible night that follows, each of the planetary intelligences—Viritrilbia (Mercury), Perelandra, Malacandra, Glund (Saturn), Lurga (Jupiter)—descends to pour its special gifts and powers into Merlin so that he may make the journey to Belbury and destroy it.

From this point on, Merlin becomes the active force of good in the novel, Mr. Fisher-King the passive. It is Merlin who goes to Belbury, confounds the scientists with the curse of Babel, releases the beasts, and prepares the destruction.

What Lewis finds in Merlin is a figure, half-mythical and half-real (in terms of Lewis' imposed theory of history which claims that the story of Arthur is historical fact), whom he can use as an active force of good and whom he can ally naturally with the Arthurian myth and artificially with the cosmic myth. Mr. Fisher-King quite obviously cannot be this active force that Lewis needs in the final chapters, since his physical wound and his passive, semidivine character would make any physical action on his part incongruous. On the other hand, none of the other characters in Mr. Fisher-King's entourage has been prepared to fulfill, or, in reality, is capable of fulfilling this function. Thus Merlin, who is, as we have seen, both a man of action and a man of magic, is the logical choice. Also, Merlin is, of course, a part of the Arthurian myth, in terms of which Lewis has been working all along. Through the device of having the planetary intelligences descend to pour their powers and influences into him, Lewis is able to connect Merlin with the silent-planet myth and thus use him, as he had used Mr. Fisher-King, within the contexts of both myths.

These elements, then, of the Arthurian myth—the figures of the Fisher King and Pendragon; the remnant of Logres; the perpetual dichotomy of Logres and Britain; and the character of Merlin—are used by Lewis in *That Hideous Strength* to present a myth that is capable of expressing in a more familiar and less overtly "unreal" form the same themes that are carried in the first two novels of the trilogy by the silent-planet myth. The Arthurian myth, at the same time, could be made to fit within the symbolic structure, already clearly defined, of that cosmic myth. The reasons that such a plan was necessary are clear. *That Hideous Strength* is a novel about people on earth; the seroni, hrossa, green goddesses, and Oyersu, all of which function perfectly on Mars and Venus, could not be forced into this new context. But Lewis could manage an extension of his myth into terms more suited to an earthly situation. The Arthurian myth could be made (through a semifictional reading of history) adaptable to a normal, albeit fictional, earthly situation, and at the same time be easily fitted through the character of Ransom to the silent-planet structure.

The question, however, of how Lewis uses the Arthurian myth remains to be answered, and it would be best to speak generally of Lewis' attitude toward myth before attempting to answer it. I have already quoted in connection with Charles Williams the most illuminating single statement that Lewis makes concerning his attitude toward myth. To Lewis, myth is "non-incarnate History," half-glimpsed truth. In another place, Lewis notes in a discussion of the Incarnation that the accounts of the death and rebirth of earlier gods seem to him to represent occurrences of "good dreams,"[14] hints of the nature of the universal and half-understood cosmic truths which are applied to local deities. Thus Lewis posits myth as a manifestation of universal reality, which is seen only in "hints and guesses" and is awaiting its final Incarnation as history. In Lewis' fiction this view of myth is graphically presented. On the planets that he visits, Ransom sees the substantive realities of what Earth men are used to think of as myth presumably, to refer again to the terms of Lewis' own myth, because mankind is cut off from the truths that the heavens hold. In *Perelandra*, Ransom suddenly finds himself near a strange tree guarded by a dragon:

> He opened his eyes and saw a strange heraldically coloured tree loaded with yellow fruits and silver leaves. Round the base of the indigo stem was coiled a small dragon covered with scales of red

gold. He recognized the garden of the Hesperides at once. (*PE* 41)

And again, in the same novel, Ransom sees strange sea-creatures swimming about:

> There—and there again—it was unmistakable: now a shoulder, now a profile, and then for one second a full face: veritable mermen or mermaids. . . . He remembered his old suspicion that what was myth in one world might be fact in some other.
> (*PE* 103–104)

Later in the novel, Ransom is told by an inner voice to kill Weston, the Un-Man, and on rebelling from the command is told "It is not for nothing that you are named Ransom."

> All in a moment of time he perceived that what was, to human philologists, a merely accidental resemblance of two sounds, was in truth no accident. The whole distinction between things accidental and things designed, like the distinction between fact and myth, was purely terrestrial. . . . Before his Mother had borne him, before his ancestors had been called Ransoms, before *ransom* had been the name for a payment that delivers, before the world was made, all these things had so stood together in eternity that the very significance of the pattern at this point lay in their coming together in just this fashion. (*PE* 153–154)

In a later scene in the novel, the Oyersu of Malacandra and Perelandra appear before him and assume shapes so that he may see them:

> The two white creatures were sexless. But he of Malacandra was masculine (not male); she of Perelandra was feminine (not female). Malacandra seemed to him to have the look of one standing armed, at the ramparts of his own remote archaic world, in ceaseless vigilance, his eyes ever roaming the earthward horizon whence his danger came long ago. . . . But the eyes of Perelandra opened,

as it were, inward, as if they were the curtained gateway to a world of waves and murmurings and wandering airs. . . . On Mars the very forests are of stone; in Venus the lands swim. For now he thought of them no more as Malacandra and Perelandra. . . . With deep wonder he thought to himself, "My eyes have seen Mars and Venus. I have seen Ares and Aphrodite." (*PE* 214–215)

In *That Hideous Strength*, when the Oyersu of the planets descend to strengthen Merlin, each manifests its identity by means of the characteristics usually associated with its mythical counterpart on earth. Thus, all of the household is possessed with "toppling structures of double meaning" and "sky rockets of metaphor and allusion" when the "lord of Meaning himself . . . whom men call Mercury and Thoth" appears (*HS* 381–382). At the coming of Venus appears Charity "fiery, bright," accompanied by a wind bearing "ponderous fragrance of night-scented flowers" (*HS* 383). Mars appears "tonic and lusty and cheerily cold" (*HS* 385); Saturn "granite-like" (*HS* 386); Jupiter with "kingship and power and festal pomp and courtesy" (*HS* 387). So in Lewis do the myths of earth reflect the realities of the spheres.

There are also indications that Lewis is using the common mythical pattern of death and rebirth to explain the transformation of Ransom into Mr. Fisher-King.[15] In the fight with Weston on Perelandra, Ransom is dragged deep underneath the sea, down to an underwater cave from which he finally makes his way back to the surface, there to rest for a "fortnight or three weeks." The period of convalescence was "a time to be remembered only in dreams as we remember infancy. Indeed it was a second infancy, in which he was breast-fed by the planet Venus herself: unweaned till he moved from that place." (*PE* 192) It is at this point that he discovers the bleeding heel wound he received in the fight with Weston which, unlike his other wounds, will not heal. After being "weaned . . . from this place of rest" (*PE* 198), he finds, significantly, that on "the third day he was well" (*PE* 201). I do not wish to overstate the case here, but it looks very much as if Lewis is using a descent and reascent pattern, mirrored here by the descent into and reascent from the cave, to explain the emergence of the new Ransom. It is significant also that he is at the point marked with the wound of the Fisher King.

Thus Lewis' general use of myth, along with his statements concerning the nature of myth, would seem to point to a unified concept of the place of myth in literature generally: Myth itself represents an ultimate and absolute reality; myth in literature represents a reflection of that reality, a shadowy and sometimes distorted reflection of that reality to be sure, but nearly always capable of conveying the meaning and, to some extent, the power implicit in the myth itself. Lewis implies both in his statements on myth and in his own allusions to myth that myth functions in literature as a suggestive archetype to which ordinary fictional situations may be referred by allusion. In this way, myth lends its own total meaning and inherent power to the fictional situation.[16]

Seen in the light of this generalization, the use of the Arthurian myth in *That Hideous Strength* becomes clear. Lewis, in adapting the Arthurian materials, is extremely selective; he concentrates, as I have said, on only a few elements of the familiar story—the Fisher King and Pendragon, Merlin, the notion of Logres as civilization. But by using these four elements, Lewis is able by indirection to imply the whole history of the Table and through this implication to suggest a comparison between Logres and modern England. To be sure, Lancelot, Guinevere, Gawain, Kay, and the rest are never mentioned, but the central conflict of Logres and Britain, the religious and the secular societies, controls and orders the Arthuriad and *That Hideous*

Strength and, though in a different context, *Till We Have Faces*. The search for grace by which the time and the civilization may be redeemed from the secular materialism of both Mordred and the N.I.C.E. is constantly implied by the presence of the Arthurian characters. Through the Arthurian myth, Lewis conveys the impression that we are dealing not merely with the moral struggles of Jane and Mark Studdock, but with issues of momentous importance, issues that once split the kingdom and destroyed the civilization whose unification could have brought about the Second Coming. The presence of the Arthurian materials thus suggests the gravity of the issue. It would have been impossible to suggest a theme of such grandeur and magnitude in terms of the battle between Bracton College and Belbury. To have discussed the theme in terms of the silent-planet myth alone would have been, as we have said, incongruous. But to place the battle within the Arthurian context magnifies and gives meaning to the theme, without removing entirely the useful eldilic machinery developed in the first two novels. The Arthurian myth, in short, gives to the fictional situation of *That Hideous Strength* the full meaning and power inherent in its own structure.

5

T. S. Eliot

So MUCH HAS been written about T. S. Eliot's literary
and philosophical development that it would seem un-
necessary to comment further on these matters. But although critics have made much of Eliot's swing from
restless poetic innovation and fierce social and religious
criticism to metrical formality and acceptance of a
tradition-bound society and church, little has been said
concerning the basic attitude, present in Eliot's work
from the beginning, which underlies and in a sense mo-
tivates these seemingly irresponsible changes. Since
this attitude has a great deal to do with Eliot's use of
myth, it will be necessary to attempt a definition of this
prevailing point of view.

I have already attempted to define the sort of mentality involved in the creation of literary myth. Basically,
the mythmaker is a primitive; he sees no division between himself and the nature that exists outside himself.
To quote again from Henri Frankfort:

> The world appears to primitive man neither in-
> animate nor empty, but redundant with life; and
> life has individuality, in man and beast and plant,
> and in every phenomenon which confronts man—
> the thunderclap, the sudden shadow, the eerie and
> unknown clearing in the wood, the stone which
> suddenly hurts him when he stumbles on a hunting
> trip. Any phenomenon may at any time face him,

not as 'It,' but as 'Thou.' In this confrontation, 'Thou' reveals its individuality, its qualities, its will. 'Thou' is not contemplated with intellectual detachment; it is experienced as life confronting life, involving every faculty of man in a reciprocal relationship.[1]

A modern version of this same attitude, it seems to me, is contained in Eliot's famous description of the unified sensibility:

When a poet's mind is perfectly equipped for its work, it is constantly amalgamating disparate experience; the ordinary man's experience is chaotic, irregular, fragmentary. The latter falls in love, or reads Spinoza, and these two experiences have nothing to do with each other, or with the noise of the typewriter or the smell of cooking; in the mind of the poet these experiences are always forming new wholes.[2]

In both instances, primitive man and modern poet, we have a point of view suggested which regards the universe as a reconcilable and unified, if not thoroughly systematic, whole. The principles of identity and reconciliation are present in both statements and represent a quality that is common to and necessary for both the mythmaker and, in Eliot's view, the poet.

This identification of mythmaker and poet seems to me to throw a good deal of light on Eliot's basic attitude toward poetry and toward the world. This point of view, which I call "sacramental," seems to me to underlie all of Eliot's work. Basically, the sacramentalist, like primitive man, can see no difference between himself and the world of natural things which surrounds him; he has, in Eliot's phrase, a "unified sensibility" that enables him to see all experience, however disparate it may first appear, as a whole and unified complex of meaning, unified because it is interpreted in terms of its relation to the whole milieu of experience by a mind that is not only cognizant of those relations, but ready and able to interpret them as they relate to one another and to his own personality. In short, the "odour of a rose," in Eliot's view, becomes a total part of Donne's experience and personality;[3] Donne unites that odor with the total complex of his experience, seen under the aspects of both time and space, of which it is a part. *Sub specie aeternitatis,* therefore, Donne is of no more importance in the total experience than is the rose that originally started the chain of reaction; they exist as equal parts of a total experience.

In addition to seeing no difference between the "I" of self and the "It" of nature, the sacramentalist also constantly identifies symbol and object. To use again the most obvious nonliterary example, there is no essential difference to a communicant who accepts the doctrine of the Real Presence in the "reality" of the actual Body and Blood of Christ and the wafer of unleavened bread and cup of wine which symbolize that Body and that Blood. No matter how the particular relationship of symbol and object is defined, whether as transubstantiation or consubstantiation, the main point, grasped and adhered to certainly by an act of faith, is that that symbol and object do exist in some sort of unity, which though certainly undefinable is nevertheless "real." Because of this, reason and thus definition cannot be used to explain the phenomenon; it is only properly felt and believed by a mentality unaccustomed, whether unconsciously or consciously, to analysis and unused to the separation of man and nature, self and nonself. This is, of course, precisely the same habit of thinking that primitive man employs when he blames the stone that he kicked for hurting him. Thus it is that the poetry of Charles Williams admits no difference in kind between the modern world and the Arthurian myth that he uses as its symbol. Thus it is that Donne is able to compare his ailing body to a map[4] and Marvell the progress of his love to a set of geometrical equations[5] with no sense of insecurity, or of unreality, or of ineptness. These poets and primitives see man and nature, seen and unseen, object and symbol as parts of a total experience, unified in spite of itself by their sacramental points of view. To them the word is made flesh at all times and on an infinite number of levels.

These two aspects of the sacramental point of view— the fusion of man and nature and of symbol and object —seem to me to underlie all of Eliot's career from "The Love Song of J. Alfred Prufrock" through "Little Gidding"; they are demonstrable in his poetry long before his conversion to Anglo-Catholicism. That he has continued them in his later religious poetry is obvious, since Eliot's current belief in the Incarnation as the unifier of all experience ("Here the impossible union / Of spheres of existence is actual")[6] has led him further from the analytical abstracting of the scientific mind than did his early theory of the dissociation of sensibility, which is primarily a matter of literary history. But even before *For Launcelot Andrewes*, the sacramental viewpoint was there, exhibiting itself in a form totally unlike that of any poet (with the possible exceptions of Coleridge and Hopkins) since the metaphysicals. This is nowhere so graphically illustrated as in the mythopoetic method of *The Waste Land*.

It is a commonplace that the secret to any interpretation of *The Waste Land* lies in an analysis of Eliot's use of myth in that poem. But more often than not this fact is singled out for scorn rather than for praise. At first glance, the poem appears chaotic, disunified; the profusion of references to myth and literature and the lack of transitional statements between the swift changes in scene give the poem a cluttered appearance. Because of this, some critics have claimed that the poem lacks any sort of unity, except perhaps for a purely artificial and mechanical unity of method and for an over-all unity of effect based on the shaky principle of imitative form.[7] This so-called "fallacy of imitative form" we can, I think, safely ignore since it is concerned only with partial effect and is not therefore really connected with any principle of total unity. The question of artificial unity of method, on the other hand, comes closer to the truth of the matter.

The mechanical unity of the poem is said to lie in Eliot's trick of setting a scene from myth or literature and a contemporary scene in close proximity and then settling back to watch the immediate effect of that comparison.[8] A good example of this method appears in the use of Tiresias in the seduction scene of "The Fire Sermon."[9] Eliot in his notes to the poem quotes a section of the *Metamorphoses* which explains two essential facts about the Greek seer—(1) he has been both man and woman and (2) he is able to know the future. Both of these miraculous qualities, moreover, are caused by his having been involved in situations involving sexual relations. He was condemned to live for seven years as a woman because he interfered with the mating of two snakes; he was privileged to see the future as compensation for the blindness imposed on him by Juno when he judged against her on a question of sexual pleasure. Thus, Tiresias "though blind, throbbing between two lives, / Old man with wrinkled female breasts, can see" and judge the sordid affair between the callous "typist home at teatime" and the vain carbuncular clerk. Passages involving Tiresias occur three times during the scene—(1) in the short introductory passage I have quoted, (2) just before the entrance of the clerk when it is said that Tiresias "perceived the scene, and foretold the rest," and (3) at the moment of intercourse when he says that he has "foresuffered all / Enacted on this same divan or bed," he who has "sat by Thebes below the wall / And walked among the lowest of the dead." Here then is a mythological figure, both man and woman, seer and prophet, set beside a cheap, effortless, and mechanical seduction, the most striking quality of which is its obvious triviality. The effect of the comparison is, to me at least,

131

immediate and overwhelming. Here is Tiresias, representing the world of myth, who knows the sexual act both as a man knows it and as a woman knows it, who has been condemned and honored for interference in sexual situations, who has been involved in the great tragedy of Oedipus, who has held communion with the tragic living and "walked among the lowest of the dead" —here is Tiresias, in whose life the sexual act has been of tremendous meaning and importance, forced to watch with disgust a sexual act that is wholly mechanical and totally void of meaning. Sexual intercourse, which in past time has driven men to war, murder, and poetry and for which men once lost the world and thought the world well lost, has become, in the contemporary waste land, a matter of routine, as mechanical as combing one's hair or placing a record on the phonograph. In short, the waste land itself is by implication devoid of meaning.

The conclusion of the scene between the typist and the clerk affords another instance of Eliot's general method. As an example of a past world in which love had meaning, Eliot here uses a scrap of a song in Goldsmith's *The Vicar of Wakefield*.[10] After the clerk has gone, the typist remarks that she is "glad it's over," and at this point appear the lines:

> When lovely lady stoops to folly and
> Paces about her room again, alone,
> She smooths her hair with automatic hand,
> And puts a record on the gramophone.
>
> (ll. 253–256)

The lines from *The Vicar of Wakefield* which Eliot is parodying begin:

> When lovely woman stoops to folly,
> And finds too late that men betray,
> What charm can soothe her melancholy?
> What art can wash her guilt away?

and conclude with the observation that the only "art her guilt to cover" is "to die." Again the contrast is immediate and overwhelming. Eliot's ironic use of this eighteenth-century lyric, and especially of the sexual connotations of "to die," expresses directly and forcefully a contrast between modern sexual ennui and an older concept of romantic honor by suggesting, in the twisting of Goldsmith's lyric, the difference between two civilizations.

I bring forward these interpretations in demonstration of a kind of unity which underlies the poem and which can be clearly demonstrated by an analysis of Eliot's method at any point in the poem. Yet it is manifestly a mechanical unity, imposed from without by an intellect extremely conscious of the trick it is using. An organic unity must, by definition, come from within the poem's elementary structure, guiding and shaping the tenor and structure of the whole poem rather than of the parts. Two comments on organic structure, in specific application to Eliot and *The Waste Land,* come immediately to mind. The first is: This organic unity must proceed out of what I have previously called a sacramental point of view that, as I have defined it, either will not or cannot see that the compared and contrasted items, no matter from where in time or space they may be drawn, are of any essential difference in kind. In short, just as Donne's comparison of the body and map or of the lovers and compass is perfectly natural to a mind used to this sort of mythopoetic thought, so must the presence of Tiresias in the room of the typist proceed not from a conscious trick of methodology but from a mind, like Donne's, which sees neither strangeness nor trickery in the comparison.

The existence of such an attitude is manifestly undemonstrable except perhaps by the method I have previously suggested, i.e., that the poet is able to work with equal ease with either set of terms involved in the comparison. Unfortunately, the comparisons introduced in *The Waste Land* are too limited in duration to allow this method. But the presence of the sacramental point of view may also be indicated by the nature of the images used by Eliot in the poem; with this matter I wish to deal in the second of these two general comments on organic unity in *The Waste Land*. The objections of those critics who give to *The Waste Land* mechanical but not organic unity may be reduced, it seems to me, to a single statement—*The Waste Land* consists of too great a variety of comparisons to have any one organically unifying principle. These critics have a point; *The Waste Land* is on first glance a hodgepodge. Yet the varying images and seemingly disconnected comparisons of *The Waste Land* may be shown to be variations of one image and one comparison, a fact that would seem to point to the presence of the sacramental point of view. That basic metaphor involves the waste land of the Arthurian myth.

Eliot's introductory note to the poem states that "not only the title, but the plan and a good deal of the incidental symbolism of the poem were suggested by Miss Jessie L. Weston's book on the Grail legend: *From Ritual to Romance*." It is almost certain, judging from Eliot's note, that he came to know the myth from Miss Weston's book. He thus saw the myth primarily from her ritualist and Celticist point of view and accepted her interpretation of the major symbols. The Fisher King–waste-land myth, according to Miss Weston's interpretation, is primarily sexual in conception and function. The Fisher King is interpreted as a symbolic representative of the life principle whose maimed condition indicates a failure in his virility; his traditional wound in the thigh becomes a symbolic castration. This wounding of the Fisher King's virility, moreover, is reflected in the blight visited upon his land. Having quoted a passage from the *Sone de Nansai* which lists among the blights that strike the waste land the facts that

Ne enfes d'omme n'e nasqui
Ne puchielle n'i ot mari
Ne arbres fueille n'i porta

Ne nus pres n'i reverdia,
Ne nus oysiaus n'i ot naon
Ne se n'i ot beste faon. . . .[11]

Miss Weston says concerning this passage:

Now there can be no possible doubt here, the condition of the King is sympathetically reflected on
the land, the loss of virility in the one brings about
a suspension of the reproductive processes of Nature on the other.[12]

According to Miss Weston, this legend, which has its
roots in fertility rituals, becomes associated in the Middle Ages with the growing body of the Arthurian materials, and the cup and lance of the older legend (both
of which are patently sexual in origin in Miss Weston's
view) become the Grail and Bleeding Lance of the
Christian story.

I have already quoted in connection with Charles
Williams, Eliot's remarks on a poet's method of operation. The gist of those remarks is that the poet is, by
nature, a man of "unified sensibility," who sees all experience, however disparate, as potential material for
art. The theory of the "objective correlative," moreover,
assumes that emotional states are transmitted not by
abstractions, but by these disparate poetic concretions
that serve in turn to evoke like states of mind in the
reader. It seems to me that Eliot finds in Miss Weston's
discussion of the Fisher King–waste-land legend a perfect objective correlative to his own generalized emotion toward contemporary society. To Eliot, the modern
world *is* a waste land, devastated by moral and spiritual
wounds that have affected its reproductive organs and
creative functions. The modern world cannot create,
cannot reproduce; it is, in essence, a dead land. In the
myth, as it exists in Miss Weston's reading, this death is
intimately connected with sterility, and it is my contention that this central image of sexual sterility forms the
underlying foundation of all the supposedly varied and
disunified metaphorical allusions in the poem. My case

for organic unity, and hence for the sacramental point of view in *The Waste Land*, therefore, lies in Eliot's use of the sterility image of the Fisher King–waste-land myth as it comes to him from Jessie Weston's *From Ritual to Romance*.

One need only glance at the wealth of exegetical studies of *The Waste Land* to realize that every detail of the poem has already been interpreted in the light of its possible connections with myth generally and with the Grail myth in particular. Grover Smith states in prefacing a complete examination of the text that "*The Waste Land* summarizes the Grail legend, not precisely in the usual order, but retaining the principal incidents and adapting them to a modern setting."[13] There is thus no need for my explicating the poem in detail. The Grail myth can be seen to underlie the poem at every point, either in images that refer directly to the myth (the protagonist's "fishing in the dull canal," the journey to the Chapel Perilous) or indirectly to the sexual sterility that, in Miss Weston's interpretation, is a vital part of the myth (the frustrated women of "A Game of Chess," the homosexual Mr. Eugenides).

The use of the Grail myth as a unifying image thus allows for the presence of the sacramental point of view in that the myth provides a kind of matrix out of which and about which all of Eliot's images, drawn from wherever or whenever, may evolve and cluster. The Arthurian myth establishes for Eliot by means of its own inclusiveness and unity the artistic equivalent of Charles Williams' "co-inherence of souls." Just as the concept of the co-inherence allows Williams to mix magical and commonplace, living and dead, so Eliot's over-all waste-land myth allows him to fuse Marvell's "Coy Mistress," Day's goddess Diana, and the exfighter Apeneck Sweeney into a single image that contains within itself the opposites of attraction and repulsion, past and present, mythical and modern and *is* itself a sacramental fusing of image and idea.

A few examples from the poem should demonstrate how the Grail myth serves to permit Eliot's sacramentalism to operate in *The Waste Land*.

The poem begins with a section "identifying the class and character of the protagonist."[14] Yet the first seven lines of the poem serve also to introduce the general theme of sexual sterility which underlies the poem, and thus prepare us for the introduction of the myth. April is generally associated with the regeneration of the earth and thus with love and birth. But in Eliot's poem, April is "cruel": "the dull roots" are stirred by the rain; the lilacs are simply "bred" out of a "dead soil" (ll. 1–7). Birth is an uncomfortable process; winter with its "forgetful snow" and "dried tubers" was sterile, yet safer than this birth-giving April. It is in this context that we first see the waste land itself:

> A heap of broken images, where the sun beats,
> And the dead tree gives no shelter, the cricket no
> relief,
> And the dry stone no sound of water. (ll. 22–24)

But even in the midst of this desert lies a hope:

> There is shadow under this red rock,
> (Come in under the shadow of this red rock).
>
> (ll. 25–26)

Under this "rock," then, exists some kind of regeneration; there is "shadow" here. The symbol of the rock is here ambivalent, referring as it does to Christ ("the shadow of a great rock in a weary land"), to the Grail itself (in Wolfram's *Parzifal*, "the Grail is said to be a stone, and those who are called to its quiet are said to be called as children and to grow up under its shadow")[15] and to Chrétien's castle of ladies, "la roche de Sanguin."[16] Thus, in the midst of images of sterility, the Grail itself is present to remind us of a kind of religious fertility and order which may revitalize the waste land.

There follow immediately in the poem two other sets of symbols referring again to this pattern of sexual sterility and demonstrating the presence of the sacramental point of view (ll. 31–42). The hopeful cry of the sailor accompanying Isolde to Cornwall and its answer, the dismal report of the shepherd who watches the empty sea for Isolde's return, are used to frame the protagonist's encounter with the hyacinth girl. The hyacinth girl, "arms full and hair wet," obviously a symbol of sexual fertility, is greeted by her lover (to Grover Smith, the Grail quester himself), who, neither "living nor dead," cannot in any way partake of her sexuality and is stunned by her vibrant life; he "knew nothing, / Looking into the heart of light, the silence." Thus, in this opening description of the waste land, Eliot presents in rapid succession an image (the red rock) which refers directly to the Grail legend and, in the Isolde and hyacinth girl sections, images that refer indirectly to the sterility-fertility dichotomy that underlies the Grail myth. This opening passage, moreover, indicates quite clearly the type of methodology and the kind of poetic mentality which pervade the poem; an image of great potential fertility drawn from whatever source (the seaman's song, the hyacinth girl) is presented and then immediately fused with a contrary image or with a denial of the original image in its own terms (the shepherd's song, the protagonist's refusal to accept the girl). The sacramental point of view, stemming from the unified sensibility, thus allows Eliot to "amalgamate disparate experience" in images that unite oppositions in time, place, and attitude.

Other images show the same process at work. In Eliot's presentation of Madame Sosostris, the fortune-teller (ll. 43–59), the Tarot deck of cards, which once played a part in ancient fertility rituals, is here seen as a mere fortunetelling device used, significantly, by a society fortuneteller who has a "cold," which is generally in Eliot a sterility symbol.[17] The characters as they appear on the cards also become symbols connected with the basic fertility-sterility image pattern that dominates the poem. The "drowned Phoenician sailor" is later connected with the Phoenician merchant who suffers "death by water" and so becomes, as Brooks suggests, a "type of the fertility god whose image was thrown into the sea annually. . . ."[18] "Belladonna [symbolically a modern poisoning of the image of the Blessed Virgin], the Lady of the Rocks" is a denial of Divine Motherhood, hence motherhood itself, in terms of the waste land. She has become simply the "lady of situations," a phrase that would seem to carry connotations of illicit sexual relationships. The "man with three staves" is associated by Eliot himself with the maimed Fisher King; the one-eyed merchant later becomes associated with the homosexual Mr. Eugenides, who represents another kind of sexual sterility; the Hanged Man of the Tarot deck is associated by Eliot with Frazer's Hanged God and so directly with Christ and indirectly with the Grail. Thus again, the emphasis of the scene is directed to the principal themes and symbols of the Fisher King myth—sexual sterility and the saving power of the Grail.

One could go on demonstrating the same point in almost every line. The fusion of the passionate fertility of myth (Cleopatra, Dido, Eve) with the frustration and sterility of modern society in "A Game of Chess," the intermingling of the various river scenes in "The Fire Sermon," the journey to the Chapel Perilous and the final images of fragmentation in "What the Thunder Said"—all of these images indicate clearly the use of the Grail myth as objective correlative and as matrix.

It should be clear also that this fusing of images within the organic unity of the poem differs from the simple mechanical unity obtained by setting past and present side by side. This latter device corresponds to the "illustrative" use of metaphor; it is a comparative device, and from this point of view the image of Tiresias in "The Fire Sermon" is simply compared with the image of clerk and typist. However, by means of the sacramental point of view the images are not compared, but identified, and in the seduction scene it will be noted that Tiresias is physically present and that he both sees the scene before him and feels (by means of his "foresuffering") the emotions of both (because of his dual sexuality) typist and clerk. Tiresias, in the poem, is not compared with the modern lovers; he is identified with them in terms of the sterility-fertility myth of which they are both a part. Eliot himself reinforces in the notes to the poem this notion of the kind of unity exhibited in the poem by stating that "just as the one-eyed merchant, seller of currants, melts into the Phoenician Sailor, and the latter is not wholly distinct from Ferdinand Prince of Naples, so all the women are one woman, and the two sexes meet in Tiresias."[19]

So in Eliot's poem, all literature and all myth become aspects of one literature and one myth. The poem's much discussed contrasts between Elizabethan England and modern England, Eastern religion and Western secular thought, fertility and sterility all exist within the context of the poem as parts and aspects of a legend and symbol that Eliot uses to control the material that goes into the making of his vision of his own time.

This use of the sacramental point of view to suggest by means of allusion whole structures and attitudes, moreover, is seen throughout Eliot's work. In four well-known lines from "Sweeney among the Nightingales," Eliot alludes in passing to four myths:

> The nightingales are singing near
> The Convent of the Sacred Heart,
>
> And sang within the bloody wood
> When Agamemnon cried aloud.

The reader, perhaps unfairly, is expected to enlarge upon each of these allusions, bringing to bear on the poem the whole weight of the full situation that each allusion suggests. He must know that the legends concerning the rape of Philomel, the Crucifixion of Christ, the murder of the priest in the sacred wood at Nemi, and the murder of Agamemnon by Aegisthus and Clytemnestra are all basically concerned with high crimes involving murder, sex, violence, and treachery. The reader must also apply this information to the text of the whole of Eliot's poem in order to understand the contrast that Eliot is enforcing, a contrast between these ancient crimes, all of which involve violence and meaning and purpose, and the proposed murder of Sweeney, which is confused and most obviously meaningless and purposeless. But, to repeat, the whole force and impact of the poem depend upon the reader's ability to supply the full meaning of the mythical situations to which Eliot merely alludes. This method is typical of Eliot's general handling of myth. A name, a place, an allusion is enough to suggest the whole situation from which the key word comes. Thus it is that in *The Waste Land* the twisted lines from Marvell and Day suggest the whole poems from which they are taken as well as the total milieu and cultural situation which produced those poems.

This reliance on myth and on the sacramental point of view may well be, as I have suggested earlier, the unifying thread that binds all of Eliot's work together. Grover Smith points out, quite conclusively it seems to me, that the mythical pattern of death and rebirth underlies almost all of Eliot's creative work,[20] and I would maintain that the sacramental method is the means whereby this pattern is presented in terms and symbols which, though they shift from work to work, are nevertheless consistent in that they constantly reflect that pattern, and that it is also the means whereby Eliot's works acquire organic unity.

Certainly, from one point of view, the earlier poems can be seen as quests, if not for the specifically Christian Grail of the Arthurian myth, then at least for the fertility and purpose and vision which the Grail symbolizes. Though it is perhaps an error to see specific allusions to the Grail myth in poems such as "The Love Song of J. Alfred Prufrock," "Mr. Apollinax," and "Gerontion," there is nevertheless demonstrated in these poems the same sacramental use of myth which determines the form and meaning of *The Waste Land*.

"Prufrock" fuses into a series of images two worlds, the world Prufrock envisions (the redeemed and fertile waste land) and the world as it is (the waste land itself). Thus the famous image of "the evening . . . spread out against the sky / Like a patient etherised upon a table" fuses Prufrock's romantic expectation (he expects the evening to be "spread out" in a magnificent fashion) with his actual perception (the etherized patient). And the same sacramental fusion is present in the images drawn from myth and literature. The socialite, culture-conscious "women" of Prufrock's own society and Michelangelo (here representing the most vigorously masculine and fertile creativity) are fused into a single image. Prufrock is ironically compared, again by means of this same kind of image, with Hamlet, with Lazarus, with John the Baptist, with Marvell's lover, and through the epigraph to the poem, with Guido de Montefeltro, all of whom represent the fertile, active, decisive life for which Prufrock is searching.

This same technique is perceptible in other early poems of Eliot. In "Mr. Apollinax," the hero, a "charming man," is sharply ridiculed by images in which he is linked, and so ironically compared, with Priapus, the old man of the sea, and the centaur. "Gerontion" defines the sterility and ineffectualness of the modern waste land by fusing images of modern sterility (the old man's house, his blindness, the sneezing woman, the hazy international set of lines 23–29, the distorted images of history, the final fragments) with images of fertility (Thermopylae, the pirates, the goat, Christ the tiger, May, passion). In "Sweeney Erect," Apeneck Sweeney, here awakening in a brothel, is identified with Polyphemus and the "epileptic on the bed" with Nausicaä. In each of these poems, the sacramental method controls both meaning and structure by yoking items of "disparate experience," all of which ultimately stem from the central image of the failure of the quest for fertile life in the midst of a sterile world.

The sacramental fusion of images is even more readily apparent in the poems, and incidentally the plays, following *The Waste Land*, though here specifically Christian images, drawn principally from Dante, St. John of the Cross, and the liturgy, take the place of the older pagan symbols. In these poems, the "still point," the point of fusion of time and timelessness, matter and spirit, man and God comes more and more to fill Eliot's mind and to dominate and so give organic unity to his poems. The image of the still point, or in specifically Christian terms the Incarnation, which appears in *Four Quartets* and in *The Family Reunion* and *Murder in the Cathedral* is itself the supreme image of the sacramental consciousness:

Here the impossible union
Of spheres of existence is actual,
Here the past and future
Are conquered and reconciled. . . .
("The Dry Salvages")

It is toward this "impossible union" that Eliot continually strives in his later work. Hence one finds in these poems an even greater clustering and fusing of images drawn from myth and literature, images that again are determined by the constant pervading and unifying influence of the death-rebirth pattern. In "Journey of the Magi," ordinary temporality is ignored as the wise men encounter images of the crucifixion ("three trees on the low sky," "six hands at an open door dicing for pieces of silver") as they approach Bethlehem. Once there, they find the "birth" to be "hard and bitter agony for [them], like Death." In "Ash Wednesday," images taken from *The Divine Comedy*, St. John

143

of the Cross, Shakespeare's sonnets, the bestiaries, the Scriptures, the liturgy, Grimm's fairy tales, and Guido Cavalcanti flow together with perfect ease to form a single unified image of penitence. Grover Smith finds in sixty lines of the "second movement" of "Little Gidding" possible allusions to Kipling, Tourneur, Shakespeare, Mallarmé, Milton, Swift, Ford, Yeats, Johnson, and Dante fused into an image "showing past time as simultaneously alive";[21] and almost any given section of *Four Quartets* would, I expect, yield similar fruit.

One might be disposed to treat such a use of allusion as mere virtuosity, a delight in erudition and obscurity for their own sakes. But it can also be seen as Eliot's attempt to make his poetry itself an image of the "impossible union / Of spheres of existence," to create within his poetry a single concentrated image of life, seen *sub specie aeternitatis,* an image distilled out of time and space by means of the sacramental point of view.

But specifically how and why does Eliot use the Arthurian myth in *The Waste Land?* It is obvious, first of all, that I cannot say as I did concerning C. S. Lewis that Eliot selects and uses parts of the myth to suggest the whole meaning of the myth. Neither can I say as I did of Charles Williams that what we have in *The Waste Land* is a complete recreation of the whole legend. On the other hand, it is perfectly clear that the symbols of the Fisher King and the waste land dominate and control the movement of the poem. One solution I would suggest is this: Eliot finds in these two symbols almost perfect objective correlatives by which he can express the emotion he feels toward the modern world. Here in the legend are symbols that express Eliot's own disillusion (this is in spite of Eliot's statements that he was never disillusioned) and disgust—the maimed ruler and the sterile land. The advantage of this particular myth lies then in the fact that it at once focuses and interprets Eliot's general feeling toward his own age. Thus, the myth Eliot adopts in *The Waste Land* becomes the sort of image to which he can transfer his emotion and by which he can express it in art.

Eliot's own remark on myth is probably the best single statement of the point of view I am attempting to define in this study. This statement may be used, furthermore, to help define Eliot's own use of the Arthurian myth in *The Waste Land*. Myth, in Eliot's terms, becomes a "way of controlling, of ordering, of giving a shape and a significance to the immense panorama of futility and anarchy which is modern history."[22] That *The Waste Land* involves as its major theme "the futility and anarchy of modern history" no one will doubt. And I have tried to show that the Fisher King–waste-land myth "is a way of controlling, of ordering, of giving a shape and a significance" to Eliot's vision. Certainly, at any rate, if this single myth and image along with the images of sterility which it naturally implies can be traced throughout the poem, then this part of the myth does in a very real sense order and control *The Waste Land*. If, however, it is objected that it is foolish to cry "order and control" in the face of such a manifestly chaotic poem as *The Waste Land*, let me retort that Eliot's own statement on myth is made apropos of what seems superficially to be one of the most obviously chaotic novels of our time—Joyce's *Ulysses*. The point is, I think, that superficial eccentricities and difficulties do not necessarily point to a central disunity. There is no "fallacy of imitative form" actually present in *The Waste Land;* there are merely superficial difficulties engendered by the difficulty of writing a poem based on many facets of a single myth and by Eliot's notion that since "our civilization comprehends great variety and complexity," the poet must seek a central order in a surface disorder, thus producing a poetry that, in Eliot's opinion, "must be difficult."[23] But in *The Waste Land*, as in *Ulysses*, the surface variants of the basic myth (the Fisher King–waste-land theme in Eliot, the Ulysses search theme in Joyce) always point inward to the central unity. All the images, like all the characters, of *The Waste Land* are in essence one image, and this single myth, embracing as it does all the variant myths of the poem, does give order, shape, and significance to Eliot's picture of modern society.

But why, again, does Eliot pick this particular myth? One answer I have already suggested; the Fisher King–waste-land myth involves not simply fertility and sterility, but more particularly religious fertility and secular sterility, a concept implicit, though undeveloped, in Chrétien, the Vulgate Cycle, and Malory. The Fisher King, at least in the later versions that connect the whole Arthurian myth with the Grail material, is the keeper of the Grail. His only cure in these legends lies in a resanctification of his person and his mission. He awaits the coming of the pure hero who can win the Grail and use it to cure him. Thus, the waste land itself becomes an image of secularism and the Fisher King an image of the failure of religion. Significantly, and this fact must have been obvious to Eliot at the time, the only cure possible for the modern world, as well as for the waste land, is religious in nature. In spite of Miss Weston's protestations, this section of the Arthurian myth is principally a homily on the destructiveness of complete secularism. Eliot himself, of course, has since said the same thing; from 1934 onward, it has become his principal text:

> If you do away with this struggle, and maintain that by tolerance, benevolence, inoffensiveness, and a redistribution or increase of purchasing power, combined with a devotion, on the part of an elite, to Art, the world will be as good as anyone could require, then you must expect human beings to become more and more vaporous.[24]
>
> . . . the struggle of our time [is] to concentrate, not to dissipate; to renew our association with traditional wisdom; to re-establish a vital con-

nexion between the individual and the race; the struggle [is], in a word, against Liberalism. . . .[25] Thus although we find Eliot preaching no direct sermons in *The Waste Land*, it is sure that the very image, the myth that guides and controls the poem, preaches the required sermon by implication. To the general reader, as to the student of Miss Weston, the Grail myth has to do first of all with religion. Talk of mystery rites is apt and pertinent (and we have no evidence that Eliot did not accept Miss Weston's theory), but the myth at heart is religious, and by virtue of this fact *The Waste Land* is a religious poem.

It will be helpful, I think, to approach this problem of myth and unity from another vantage point. The difficulties of the poem occur not, as some critics maintain, from Eliot's failure to unite the various cultures he draws upon, but from a misunderstanding of Eliot's attitude toward the whole problem of unification. Eliot's purpose is certainly not to foster a belief in the various myths he uses. Although the great variety of myths involved hinders a superficial reading of the poem, it does not negate the possibility that the poem has unity or that it represents more than a chaos of unassimilated knowledge and impression. Myth is in itself a way of ordering knowledge, of stating precisely what the poet feels to be the state of modern society, and it is altogether possible that this "way of ordering knowledge" becomes not only the principal device of the poem, but one of its major themes as well. As in "Sweeney among the Nightingales," Eliot is involved in contrasting both the modern world in which nothing has meaning with a world where all actions have meaning and, at the same time, the secular viewpoint that sees no meaning in action with his own sacramental point of view that sees meaning in all things. Thus, the myths in *The Waste Land* may very well have a double function; they may serve not only to contrast the fertile religious order of the past with the sterile secular chaos of the present, but also to contrast the modern dissociation of matter and form with the poet's own viewpoint that asserts the inseparability of matter and form. *The Waste Land* not only opposes spiritual life-in-death with secular death-in-life, but also a sacramental habit of thought with a dissociated sensibility that forbids any assimilation of experience. Seen in this light, Eliot's own attitude toward the poem becomes clear. The myths themselves may be of less importance in the poem than the attitude toward myth which unites them; Eliot everywhere suggests through his use of myth a consistent world viewpoint capable of uniting these mythical elements of the poem in contrast to a modern world view that sees all experience as disjunctive. There are thus two sets of contrasts in *The Waste Land:* a contrast of order and chaos and a contrast of the sacramental and whole world view with the secularized and partial world view.

The sacramental point of view that can equate evening and etherized patient in "The Love Song of J. Alfred Prufrock" can be seen identifying the fire and the rose in "Little Gidding"; Eliot's sacramental viewpoint orders and controls his poetry throughout his career. *The Waste Land,* moreover, would seem to be a *locus classicus* of this particular sort of method and mentality. Here, Eliot, beginning with a single myth and a single image, is able to expand that myth and that image in all directions, seeing applications of the basic principle in many times and literatures, yet never losing the single thread of imagery which controls and unifies all the subsidiary imagery of the poem. The Fisher King–waste-land section of the Arthurian myth, involving as it does religious fertility and secular sterility, thus becomes the center of Eliot's poem. In a sense, then, the Arthurian myth assumes in Eliot, just as it does in Williams and Lewis, a position of central importance.

6

Logres in Britain

IN THIS STUDY I have attempted to do two things—(1) to formulate a theory of the function of myth in literature and (2) to test that theory by applying it to the use made of one particular myth, the Arthurian, by three contemporary British writers. The theory of myth presented is simple: Myth (a form of symbolic and ordering ritual action) is the product of the primitive mentality, which, since it works by association rather than by logic, sees no difference between external reality and the symbol that it creates to represent that reality. Thus, the language used in myth is chiefly distinguished by its fusion of metaphorical and logical terms, of words that symbolize reality and words that designate real things. For example, Henri Frankfort says in *The Intellectual Adventure of Ancient Man* that the Babylonians explained the sudden appearance of a rainstorm by stating that the bird Imdugud covered the sky with its black wings and "devoured the Bull of Heaven, whose hot breath had scorched the crops."[1] We today should say that this myth effectively symbolizes the appearance of black storm clouds and the subsequent disappearance of hot, destructive winds. But this statement would be meaningless to ancients who recognized no distinction between discursive and metaphorical knowledge, to whom the great bird and the destructive bull were as real as the birds and bulls of daily experience. In short, the language of myth proceeds simultaneously on two levels of discourse, using the terms of both indiscriminately. To the primitive mythmaker, there can be no distinction between symbol and object in the poem, between what critics today call vehicle and tenor, texture and structure.

It is an integral part of my thesis that this same sacramental point of view may be observed in sophisticated modern authors as well as in untutored primitive mythmakers. The presence of such a mentality, it seems to me, is discernible in the structure of metaphorical language. The nonsacramentalist poet states his point and then proceeds to illustrate it in metaphorical terms. The sacramentalist poet, on the other hand, can make an identification of symbol and object so complete that the dialectic of the poem may proceed in either symbolic or denotative terms, in the language of either vehicle or tenor.

The effect of such an identification is that it serves to bring together into poetic unity two kinds of experience and knowledge—the concrete, though chaotic, experience of the world about us and the poet's ordered remaking of that experience within the poem. When Gerard Manley Hopkins identifies a falcon with Christ in "The Windhover," he is attempting to order and control his generalized conception of the nature of the Incarnation by casting it into terms that are more effectively and easily handled because more concrete. The use of myth as image, however, carries this process of identification one step further. The validity of the identification of the falcon and Christ in Hopkins' poem depends entirely upon Hopkins' success in formulating and communicating to the reader those qualities of the bird which permit that identification. In short, the metaphorical identification not only has no meaning outside the poem, but its existence even within the poem depends upon the skill of the poet in demonstrating to the reader upon just what qualities of the compared terms the identification rests. Myth, however, carries with it into an image a pattern of meaning already complete and ordered within itself. The poet thus brings into contact not simply two items, but two whole worlds of experience. Since myth used as image brings with it the complexity of its own whole meaning, which becomes free to operate on its own terms within the poem, the poet can use an allusion to myth to call forth the whole substance and meaning of the myth. Thus, the poet is able to superimpose the already ordered experience contained within the framework of the myth upon the chaotic experience that he is attempting to order within the poem, and by this action control and regulate his own vision of contemporary life.

The three writers with whom this study deals attempt to use the Arthurian myth, which they consider to be a primarily religious myth, for exactly this purpose. Charles Williams finds in the Arthurian myth an "objective correlative" perfectly adapted to his particular conceptions of the nature of society and religion. In his early novels, Williams attempted, somewhat unsuccessfully, I think, to embody his major themes—hierarchal order, Exchange, Beatrician love, the Ways of Affirmations and Rejections—in a series of "spiritual thrillers," tales in which these themes were reflected in the imposition of supernatural disturbances upon ordinary life. It seems certain, however, that Williams found in the Arthurian myth a literary vehicle capable of carrying easily within its predetermined structure these themes that could not be made to fit with ease into novels concerning daily life in contemporary England. Moreover, by placing his main emphasis on the Grail quest section of the myth and by envisioning the whole myth as the story of a civilization destroyed by its failure to act upon religious rather than secular values, Williams is able to identify the failures of the Arthurian civilization with those of his own; in describing the failure of Arthurian order, Williams is expressing his concern at the dissolution of religious values in his own time. The themes of Williams' remade Arthurian myth thus stem from and are reapplicable to contemporary problems. It is clear that Williams could never have succeeded in expressing these themes directly in terms of a contemporary setting; his early novels, it seems to me, are partial failures for just this reason. It is almost an axiom of literary criticism that a person can never see his own age in true perspective; only through metaphorical terms does it become whole; only then can he see it objectively. The Arthurian myth, in Williams' poetry, allows him to order and control his vision of modern society; through myth he is able to give symmetry to his world view to an extent and with a completeness impossible in a contemporary metaphor. In this way, Williams uses the order, coherence, and meaning inherent in the Arthurian myth to control his vision of contemporary life.

Much the same thing can be said of C. S. Lewis. In *That Hideous Strength*, Lewis abstracts from the Arthurian myth certain leading symbols—the Fisher King, Merlin, the remnant of Logres, the battle between Logres and "mere Britain"—which he uses to imply the whole meaning and history of the Round Table in order, like Williams, to suggest a comparison between the Arthurian world and his own age. Yet Lewis' technique in using myth differs widely from Williams'. Williams had recreated the entire myth; he had used the history of Arthur's kingdom as a gigantic image in order to formulate a sense of his own time. Lewis, on the other hand, writes a novel about his own age into which he introduces elements of the Arthurian myth. By this method, Lewis uses the myth to elevate the story of the conversion of two young moderns into an allegory of the cosmic and universal battle between good and evil. By using elements of the Arthurian myth, Lewis gives to the fictional situation of *That Hideous Strength* the high seriousness and order inherent in the structure of the myth.

It is possible to see in the work of T. S. Eliot yet another aspect of the function of myth as literary image. Instead of recreating the entire myth as does Williams, or abstracting from the myth symbols that may be used to imply the whole meaning of the myth as does Lewis, Eliot concentrates on one aspect of the myth—the religious fertility-secular sterility theme of the Fisher King–waste-land myth—in order to find an "objective correlative" to his concept of the destructiveness of the secularism of our time. Eliot's use of myth differs in technique also from Williams' and Lewis'. Eliot constantly fuses into single images allusions both to myth and to the contemporary scene in order to form ironic identifications of the fertile life of the past with the grim sterility of the present. Moreover, Eliot's sacramental images give unity to his poems since all his highly complex and apparently disconnected images are in reality aspects of one single image and theme. In *The Waste Land*, for example, although Eliot uses allusions from a great variety of myths, all these images stem from the central image of the Arthurian waste land. By means of these images Eliot is able to contrast the total cultural situations that the myths reflect with his own civilization.

Thus, although each of these writers uses a different technique in selecting and handling myth in his writings, it can be maintained that each uses myth for the same general purpose, in Eliot's terms as "a way of controlling, of ordering, of giving a shape and a significance to the immense panorama of futility and anarchy which is modern history."[2] Each uses myth to frame and thus order his conception of the world in which he lives.

This study would not be complete without some attempt at evaluation. To what degree and with what success do these writers reflect and judge the age in which they live? It should be apparent that all three writers are extremely learned men; they do not fit well into a literary milieu in which even the most serious writers—say, Hemingway, Faulkner, and Arthur Miller —have little more than professional training. They thus do not mirror, or at least only in passing, the immediate and naturalistic problems and pseudorealistic techniques that have occupied most writers in this "age of the common man." They have little to say about the latest trends and fashions in man's economic life, in his political life, or even (except in general and symbolic terms) in his sexual life. There are no crap games, "fixed" elections, or sleeping bags in Williams, Lewis, and Eliot. The names of Freud and Marx are almost conspicuously absent.

But this is not to say that these men are not modern writers in the truest sense. If they sometimes lack the immediacy and excitement of *The Man with the Golden Arm* and *From Here to Eternity*, they also rise above that immediacy. Our particular twentieth-century problems are thus presented in Williams, Lewis, and Eliot, but they are not presented in the usual twentieth-century terms. Our contemporary dilemmas and frustrations are seen by these men in relation to the universal issues of morality and religion of which they are parts, and they are presented in terms that are meaningful to all men at all times. And by means of this sort of aesthetic distance, these writers achieve not less, but more relevance to their own age.

Certainly, for example, no one would deny that these men are concerned with marriage. *Shadows of Ecstasy, All Hallows' Eve, The Greater Trumps*, Williams' Arthurian poetry, *That Hideous Strength*, and *The Cocktail Party* all have as a principal theme the relationship of husband and wife in the contemporary world. Yet the manner of presentation and, more important, the terms in which the problem is defined and settled

154

are not in themselves limited by the contemporary setting. The tormented lovers in *The Sun Also Rises, Sanctuary,* and *All the King's Men* are conditioned and shaped by a set of historical circumstances, and they react to their problems by means of fixed patterns of behavior dictated by their times. They do not rise above Freudian or Marxian patterns; they sink into them. On the other hand, Mark and Jane Studdock in *That Hideous Strength* discover in the ancient idea of natural hierarchy a principle that allows them to rise above twentieth-century moral expediency into a genuinely universal concept of the married state which is theologically as well as morally sound.

Thus, I should expect the reputations of these men to increase as the public grows progressively less dazzled by the surface realism of most popular writing. Time will surely raise Charles Williams above Sinclair Lewis, and in a sense T. S. Eliot already beacons from the abode where the eternal are. I would judge also that those works of each which are now most popular because of their bizarre devices will in time be judged least important. *Descent into Hell, All Hallows' Eve,* and Williams' Arthurian poetry will, by virtue of their universality, rank above the early theological thrillers. *That Hideous Strength* and *Till We Have Faces* will outlive *Out of the Silent Planet* and *Perelandra.*

In short, those works of each will live which present their clearest visions of the modern world, no matter how far these works may seem on their surface levels to be removed from that world. And the visions of these three writers are remarkably similar. Certainly writing as these men do, from a commonly shaped Christian point of view, each maintains the same basic attitude toward his age. Each sees the unified religious convictions of former times usurped by a growing secularism. Each seeks to return to the religious values symbolized by the Grail quest, to find some means of redeeming the time. In Charles Williams, this desire takes the form of a plea for universal charity, for a social code based on the Pauline conception of divine love. C. S. Lewis would seem to advocate a return to doctrinaire orthodoxy, to the principles and practice of the historic Church. Both practice what Williams called the Way of Affirmations. The third, T. S. Eliot, follows the Way of Rejections. After *The Waste Land*, Eliot's work has retreated farther and farther from the world into the mystical vision. And even though *The Cocktail Party* and *The Confidential Clerk* allow for the way of the world and the troublesome, noisy existences of ordinary men, these plays are nevertheless the products of that vision, reflecting as they do Eliot's interest in the ascetic life of the saint.

In spite of these differences, however, these writers are three of the most influential interpreters of the modern world. All have succeeded in analyzing with severity and acuteness the dilemma of modern man, separated from the traditions that bind him to the past, living from day to day in uncertainty. Each, in imposing the order of myth upon the disorder of his age, has suggested a way out of the contemporary waste land.

Notes

CHAPTER 1.

[1] *Kenyon Review*, XI, 3 (Summer, 1949), 455.

[2] *Herman Melville* (New York: Macmillan, 1949).

[3] *A Motif-Index of Folk Literature* (Bloomington: Indiana University Press, 1932———).

[4] *The American Adam* (Chicago: University of Chicago Press, 1955).

[5] *Archetypal Patterns in Poetry* (London: Oxford University Press, 1934).

[6] *Hamlet and Oedipus* (New York: Norton, 1949).

[7] *The Idea of a Theatre* (Princeton: Princeton University Press, 1949).

[8] *The Burning Fountain: A Study in the Language of Symbolism* (Bloomington: Indiana University Press, 1954).

[9] "The Saturnalian Pattern in Shakespeare's Comedies," *Sewanee Review*, LIX, 4 (Autumn, 1951).

[10] For surveys of myth studies, the reader is directed to Richard Chase's *Quest for Myth* (Baton Rouge: Louisiana State University Press, 1949) and the Myth Symposium of *The Journal of American Folklore*, LVIII, 4 (Oct., 1955).

[11] "An Excursus on the Ritual Forms Preserved in Greek Tragedy," contained in Jane Harrison's *Themis* (Cambridge: Cambridge University Press, 1912), pp. 341–363.

[12] *The Origin of Attic Comedy* (London: Edward Arnold, 1914).

[13] *Zeus* (Cambridge: Cambridge University Press, 1925).

[14] *From Ritual to Romance* (Cambridge: Cambridge University Press, 1920).

[15] *Jocasta's Crime* (London: Methuen, 1933).

[16] *The Hero* (London: Methuen, 1936).

[17] *The Fool* (New York: Farrar and Rinehart, 1936).

[18] *The Hero with a Thousand Faces* (New York: Pantheon Books, 1949), p. 30.

[19] "The Archetypes of Literature," *Kenyon Review*, XIII (Winter, 1951), 92–110.

[20] *The Myth of the State* (New Haven: Yale University Press, 1946), p. 45.

[21] *Language and Myth,* tr. Susanne K. Langer (New York: Harper, 1946), p. 63.

[22] *Ibid.,* p. 18.

[23] *The Intellectual Adventure of Ancient Man* (Chicago: University of Chicago Press, 1946), p. 6.

[24] *Ibid.,* p. 3.

[25] Susanne Langer, *Philosophy in a New Key* (Cambridge, Mass.: Harvard University Press, 1942), p. 176.

[26] *The Intellectual Adventure of Ancient Man,* pp. 12–13.

[27] Coleridge's most celebrated discussion of the poetic Imagination is contained in chapter 14 of the *Biographia Literaria.*

[28] " 'Ulysses,' Order, and Myth," *Dial,* LXXV, 5 (Nov., 1923), 483.

Chapter 2.

[1] Quoted by Susanne Langer, *Philosophy in a New Key* (Cambridge, Mass.: Harvard University Press, 1942), p. 177 n.

[2] *Ibid.,* pp. 181–182.

[3] James Douglas Bruce, *The Evolution of Arthurian Romance* (Baltimore: The Johns Hopkins Press, 1923), I, 20.

[4] The tradition that Arthur retired to Avalon is mentioned first by Wace, who does no more than mention that the Britons expect his return, and first developed by Layamon, who supplies the details of Arthur's passing. But this tradition, it seems to me, in no way fulfills the requirement that the legendary hero actually return bearing gifts to his people.

[5] *A Study of History* (New York: Oxford University Press, 1934), III, 248.

[6] Charles Williams in *Arthurian Torso, containing the posthumous fragment of* The Figure of Arthur *by Charles Williams and a commentary on the Arthurian poems of Charles Williams* by C. S. Lewis (London: Oxford University Press, 1948), p. 84.

[7] J. D. Bruce, *op. cit.,* I, 250. See also pages 247–252 for a good general discussion crediting Chrétien with the invention of the characters, the quest motif, and a good many of the details of the *Conte del Graal.*

[8] *Ibid.,* I, 251.

[9] In *Studies on the Legend of the Holy Grail* (London: Harrison, 1888) and various other writings.

[10] Principally in *The Origin of the Grail Legend* (Cambridge, Mass.: Harvard University Press, 1943).

[11] In *Celtic Myth and Arthurian Romance* (New York: Columbia University Press, 1937) and *Arthurian Tradition and Chrétien de Troyes* (New York: Columbia University Press, 1949).

[12] *Op. cit.,* p. 448.

[13] *"Au Sujet du Graal,"* Romania, LXVI (1940–41), 289–321.

[14] See Miss Weston's two volumes on the subject: *The Quest of the Holy Grail* (London: G. Bell, 1913) and *From Ritual to Romance* (Cambridge: Cambridge University Press, 1920).

[15] See W. A. Nitze, "The Fisher King in the Grail Romances," *PMLA*, XXIV (1909) and various other articles.

[16] *Ibid.*, p. 366.

[17] *Quest*, p. 95.

[18] See J. D. Bruce, Vol. I, pages 269–276, for a general summary of the theory of Christian origin.

[19] Urban T. Holmes, Jr., "A New Interpretation of Chrétien's *Conte del Graal*," *University of North Carolina Studies in the Romance Languages and Literatures*, No. 8 (1948). Professor Holmes has recently suggested more evidence for his general theory in a monograph entitled "Dominican Rite and the Judaeo-Christian Theory of the Grail," published as No. 12 in the same North Carolina series. See also Sister M. Amelia Klenke, O. P., "Liturgy and Allegory in Chrétien's *Perceval*," *University of North Carolina Studies in the Romance Languages and Literatures*, No. 14 (1951).

[20] Holmes, "New Interpretation," p. 13.

[21] *Ibid.*, p. 14.

[22] See my "Malory's Treatment of the Sankgreall," *PMLA*, LXXI, 3 (June, 1956), for a full account of Malory's use of the Grail sources.

[23] See Mary E. Dichmann, "Characterization in Malory's *Tale of Arthur and Lucius*," *PMLA*, LXV (Sept., 1950), 877–895.

Chapter 3.

[1] *Arthurian Torso, containing the posthumous fragment of* The Figure of Arthur *by Charles Williams and a commentary on the Arthurian poems of Charles Williams* by C. S. Lewis (London: Oxford University Press, 1948). All page references in the text to this volume are marked *AT*.

[2] I would assume that the sections on the Cult of the Grail and on courtly love would have gone into Williams' proposed chapter 4— "The Great Inventions."

[3] "Introduction" to *The English Poems of John Milton*, "The World's Classics" (London: Oxford University Press, 1940), p. ix.

[4] *The Forgiveness of Sins* (London: Faber, 1950), p. 126.

[5] *The Allegory of Love* (Oxford: Oxford University Press, 1936), pp. 2–3.

[6] *Ibid.*, p. 25.

[7] *He Came Down from Heaven* (London: Faber, 1950), pp. 71–72.

[8] "Malory and the Grail Legend," *Dublin Review*, 429 (Apr., 1944), 146.

[9] *Ibid.*, p. 151.

[10] All the poetry of Charles Williams under discussion in this chapter is contained in two collections—*Taliessin Through Logres* and *The Region of the Summer Stars*—published in one volume by the Oxford University Press in 1955. These poems are part of a cycle of Arthurian lyrics left unfinished by the poet. All page references in the text to these collections are marked *TTL* and *SS* respectively. There are a few early Arthurian poems contained in *Heroes and Kings* (1930) and in *Three Plays* (1931), but as these poems are substantially re-

worked in the later volumes and are extremely hard to come by, they had best be omitted from the discussion here.

In limiting this study to a consideration of the use of myth in Williams, I am forced to pass over many interesting and important aspects of Williams' poetry. For example, a very fruitful study might be made of the Arthurian poems in terms of Williams' use of his sources. Williams' principal source is, of course, Malory, but he uses also older versions of the legend, and a consideration of his modifications of and additions to these sources would shed light on Williams' poetry. Yet another valuable approach to the poetry might be that of comparing Williams' prose discussions of the Arthuriad (principally *The Figure of Arthur,* but also "Malory and the Grail Legend" and the other essays and notes collected in *The Image of the City and Other Essays,* ed. Anne Ridler [Oxford: Oxford University Press, 1958], pp. 169–194) with their poetic counterparts. However, this present organization, even though it must neglect much of value, would seem to have some merit in that it examines the poetry in terms of a unified method and point of view and in that it deals with a central critical problem.

[11] See Boethius' statement that "nam sicut scientia praesentium rerum nihil his quae fiunt, ita praescientia futurorum nihil his quae ventura sunt necessitatis importat" (*Da consolatione philosophiae,* ed. H. F. Steward, "Loeb Classical Library" [New York: Putnam, 1926], p. 386). The fifth book of *The Consolation of Philosophy* is an extended discussion of this problem.

[12] *He Came Down from Heaven,* p. 20.

[13] *Ibid.,* p. 36.

[14] *Ibid.,* p. 17.

[15] *The Forgiveness of Sins,* p. 108.

[16] *He Came Down from Heaven,* p. 35.

[17] *Ibid.,* p. 25.

[18] *Ibid.,* p. 83.

[19] *Ibid.,* p. 86.

[20] *Ibid.,* p. 100.

[21] *Ibid.*

[22] Charles Williams, *The Figure of Beatrice* (London: Faber, 1943), p. 8.

[23] *The Descent of the Dove* (London: Faber, 1939), p. 58.

[24] Charles Williams, *Descent into Hell* (London: Faber, 1937). All page references in the text to this edition are marked *DIH.*

[25] "Hamlet," *Selected Essays: 1917–1932* (New York: Harcourt, Brace, 1932), pp. 124–125.

[26] Nathan Comfort Starr, *King Arthur Today* (Gainesville: University of Florida Press, 1954), p. 166. Anne Ridler's preface to *The Image of the City* shows clearly that Williams had begun pondering the Arthurian myth as early as 1912, but the selections from Williams' Commonplace Book which are reprinted on pages 169–175 of *The Image of the City* demonstrate that Williams' early conceptions of the myth did not involve the ideas that later became the burden of the finished poems. The first systematic account of Williams' reworking of the myth (though it does not agree in detail with the finished

poems) is reprinted on pages 175–179 of *The Image of the City* as "Notes on the Arthurian Myth" and is dated by the editor in the late twenties or early thirties.

[27] Anne Ridler's dating of the final versions of a number of the individual poems of the cycle during the years 1934–1936 (*The Image of the City*, p. lxiii n.) would seem to support this hypothesis.

[28] C. S. Lewis, *Miracles* (London: Geoffrey Bles, 1947), p. 161 n.

[29] *The Intellectual Adventure of Ancient Man* (Chicago: University of Chicago Press, 1946), p. 3.

CHAPTER 4.

[1] *Mere Christianity* (London: Geoffrey Bles, 1952), p. 45.

[2] *Ibid.*, p. 78.

[3] *Ibid.*, p. 76.

[4] In *The Abolition of Man* (London: Geoffrey Bles, 1943).

[5] In *The Problem of Pain* (London: Geoffrey Bles, 1940).

[6] In *Miracles* (London: Geoffrey Bles, 1947).

[7] *Till We Have Faces* (London: Geoffrey Bles, 1956), p. 182.

[8] *Ibid.*, p. 287.

[9] This Lewis does also in the "Narnia" novels, a series of "fairy stories" (though not necessarily children's books), which, like the works of his friend, Professor J. R. R. Tolkien—*The Hobbit* and the three-volume *The Lord of the Rings*—attempts to present basic Christian teachings in such a manner as to strip them "of their stained-glass and Sunday School associations" and thus reveal them in their "real potency" (C. S. Lewis, "On Fairy Stories," *New York Times Book Review* [November 18, 1956], p. 3).

[10] *Mere Christianity*, p. 37.

[11] *Out of the Silent Planet* (New York: Macmillan, 1943), p. 70. All page references in the text to this edition are marked *SP*.

[12] *Perelandra* (New York: Macmillan, 1944), p. 125. All page references in the text to this edition are marked *PE*.

[13] *That Hideous Strength* (New York: Macmillan, 1946), p. 37. All page references in the text to this edition are marked *HS*.

[14] *Mere Christianity*, p. 40.

[15] It is well to remember here that Lewis has said that the death-rebirth pattern may well be the "very formula of reality" (*Miracles*, p. 151).

[16] In this connection, C. S. Lewis has written me explaining the use of several pseudomythological figures that appear in *That Hideous Strength*: "The VII Bears [of Logres] and the *Atlantean Circle* are pure inventions of my own, filling the same purpose in narrative that 'noises off' would in a stage play. *Numinor* is my misspelling of *Numenor* which, like the 'true West,' is a fragment from a vast private mythology invented by Professor J. R. R. Tolkien" (later published, at least in part, as *The Lord of the Rings*). Lewis' statement that these "inventions" fill "the same purpose in narrative that 'noises off' would in a stage play" indicates another aspect of Lewis' use of myth. Elements of this "private mythology" are used in the novel to supply a suitable magical background for the meeting of

Merlin and Mr. Fisher-King. Thus, Lewis would seem to believe that myth may, in certain cases, function as a sort of background imagery like that described in my first chapter, which serves to create and sustain a mood and effect by reference to what appears to be a whole myth.

CHAPTER 5.

[1] *The Intellectual Adventure of Ancient Man* (Chicago: University of Chicago Press, 1946), p. 6.

[2] "The Metaphysical Poets," *Selected Essays: 1917–1932* (New York: Harcourt, Brace, 1932), p. 247.

[3] *Ibid.*

[4] In *A Hymn to God, My God, in My Sickness.*

[5] In *The Definition of Love.*

[6] "The Dry Salvages," *Four Quartets* (New York: Harcourt, Brace, 1943), p. 27.

[7] See especially Yvor Winters' condemnation of this theory in connection with Eliot that "modern art must be chaotic in order to express chaos." According to Winters, who denies any unity to *The Waste Land,* imitative form in the poem results only in confusion (*The Anatomy of Nonsense* [Norfolk: New Directions, 1943], pp. 163–165).

[8] This opinion is upheld most effectively by Edmund Wilson, who finds in Eliot's apparent fragmentariness a certain proportion and order (*Axel's Castle* [New York: Scribner, 1931], p. 112). Although Cleanth Brooks in his excellent analysis (*Modern Poetry and the Tradition* [Chapel Hill: University of North Carolina Press, 1939], pp. 136–172) treats the problem of unity only by implication, he would seem to find some unity in the poet's use of irony and "the obverse of irony" as reflected in Eliot's method of contrasting myth and contemporary reality. Other critics (see note 7 above on Yvor Winters) find that Eliot's poetic method has not even mechanical unity. Stephen Spender complains that Eliot's greatest weakness is his "fragmentariness" (*The Destructive Element* [Boston: Houghton Mifflin, 1936], p. 154). F. R. Leavis finds that the "comprehensiveness" of *The Waste Land* has been achieved at the "cost of structure" (*New Bearings in English Poetry* [London: Chatto and Windus, 1932], p. 112). This same criticism lies at the base of Richard Chase's comment that Eliot's prose statement that myth is an ordering device "is constantly belied by his use of myth in his own poems" (*Quest for Myth* [Baton Rouge: Louisiana State University Press, 1949], pp. v–vi).

[9] All the quotations from Eliot's poetry other than *Four Quartets* are taken from the American edition of the *Collected Poems, 1909–1935* (New York: Harcourt, Brace, 1936). As far as I know, none of the materials that I have used in explication are original with me, nor can I always be sure from what commentaries they are taken. The fullest explications of *The Waste Land* are those of F. O. Matthiessen in *The Achievement of T. S. Eliot* (New York: Oxford University Press, 1947), Cleanth Brooks in *Modern Poetry and the Tradition,*

and Grover Smith, Jr. in *T. S. Eliot's Poetry and Plays* (Chicago: University of Chicago Press, 1956). Smith's notes contain a full bibliography of the important commentaries on the poem.

[10] Although in *The Waste Land*, Eliot's point of reference to past glories includes both literary and mythological allusions, it is clear that they fulfill exactly the same function in that both are used to suggest total situations or milieus that can be compared to the modern waste land.

[11] Nor was any child of man born there,
Nor was any maiden married there,
Nor did the trees there bear leaves,
Nor any meadow blossom,
Nor did any birds bear young,
Nor any beast faun.

[12] *From Ritual to Romance* (Cambridge: Cambridge University Press, 1920), p. 21.

[13] *Op. cit.*, p. 70.

[14] Brooks, *op. cit.*, p. 139.

[15] Maynard Mack *et al.*, *Modern Poetry*, "English Masterpieces" Series (New York: Prentice-Hall, 1950), p. 124.

[16] Smith, *op. cit.*, p. 73.

[17] See "Gerontion": "The goat coughs at night in the field overhead." The goat is normally a fertility symbol.

[18] *Op. cit.*, p. 142.

[19] *Collected Poems*, p. 94.

[20] *Op. cit.*, *passim*.

[21] *Op. cit.*, p. 284.

[22] "'Ulysses,' Order, and Myth," *Dial*, LXXV, 5 (Nov., 1923), 483.

[23] "The Metaphysical Poets," p. 248.

[24] *After Strange Gods* (New York: Harcourt, Brace, 1934), p. 46.

[25] *Ibid.*, p. 53.

CHAPTER 6.

[1] (Chicago: University of Chicago Press, 1946), p. 6.

[2] "'Ulysses,' Order, and Myth," *Dial*, LXXV, 5 (Nov., 1923), 483.